T0300703

THE POLYAMORY BREAKUP BOOK

Also by Kathy Labriola

The Jealousy Workbook
Exercises and Insights for Managing Open Relationships

Love in Abundance
A Counselor's Advice on Open Relationships

Polyamorous Elders
Aging in Open Relationships

THE POLYAMORY BREAKUP BOOK

Causes, Prevention, and Survival

Kathy Labriola
with a foreword by Dossie Easton

THORNAPPLE
PRESS

The Polyamory Breakup Book:
Causes, Prevention, and Survival

Copyright ©2019 by Kathy Labriola

All rights reserved. No part of this book may be used or reproduced in any manner whatsoever without written permission from the publisher except in the case of brief quotations in critical articles and reviews.

Thornapple Press
300 – 722 Cormorant Street
Victoria, BC V8W 1P8 Canada
press@thornapplepress.ca

Thornapple Press is a brand of Talk Science to Me Communications Inc. and the successor to Thorntree Press. Our business offices are located in the traditional, ancestral and unceded territories of the ləkʷəŋən and W̱SÁNEĆ peoples.

Cover illustration and design by Brianna Harden
Interior design by Jeff Werner
Copy-editing by Tonya Martin
Proofreading by Hazel Boydell
Indexing by Maria Hypponen
Interior illustrations © Lacey Johnson 2019

Library of Congress Cataloging-in-Publication Data
  Names: Labriola, Kathy, author.
  Title: The polyamory breakup book : causes, prevention, and survival
    / by Kathy Labriola, with a foreword by Dossie Easton.
  Description: Portland, OR : Thorntree Press, [2019] |
  Identifiers: LCCN 2019008974 (print) | LCCN 2019010232 (ebook) |
    ISBN 9781944934828 (ebook) | ISBN 9781944934835 (kindle) |
    ISBN 9781944934842 (pdf) | ISBN 9781944934811 (pbk.)
  Subjects: LCSH: Nonmonogamous relationships. | Separation
    (Psychology) | Rejection (Psychology)
  Classification: LCC HQ980 (ebook) | LCC HQ980 .L33 2019 (print) |
    DDC 306.84/23--dc23
  LC record available at https://lccn.loc.gov/2019008974

10 9 8 7 6 5 4 3 2

Printed in the United States of America.

This book is dedicated to Ms. A. LaVigna, my eighth grade English teacher, who told me I would be a writer, and to Mr. James Martin, my tenth grade English teacher, who told me I would be a writer. I didn't believe either of them, but somehow, fifty years later, I accidentally became a writer.

Contents

Acknowledgments

I owe a special thanks to my life partners, Eric and Ricky. Each of them has generously given up receiving some of my time and attention so that I could focus on completing this book. They have been my strongest supporters and given me love, encouragement, ice cream, neck rubs, and smiles whenever things were challenging.

And I send my heartfelt gratitude to Eve Rickert and Thorntree Press, who believed in this book and took a chance on me and on publishing this book. Eve worked with me over a period of two years throughout every stage of the writing, editing, and publishing process. Thanks, Eve, for your patience, skill, and wisdom in "midwifing" this book to completion and publication!

In addition, I would like to thank Samantha Manewitz, LCSW, for assisting with the writing and editing of the section on abusive relationships, in Chapter 5. Her help dramatically improved this section, and for that, I am very grateful.

I want to send a big shout out and thank you to Lacey Johnson, the artist who created the beautiful and funny illustrations for the book. As soon as I saw Lacey's terrific zine, *Green-Eyed Monsters: My Report on Jealousy*, I immediately knew what was wrong with my first two books: no cartoons! What was I thinking? I was hooked on her comics and zines, and I knew I wanted her illustrations in my new book. Thanks, Lacey!

Last but definitely not least, I owe a huge debt of gratitude to the 45 people who allowed me to interview them for this book. They generously gave me their time and bravely bared their souls to tell me their stories about very painful breakups of polyamorous relationships. Each person described a unique set of circumstances and each experienced their own journey. However, what they went through and what they learned helped me glean some useful lessons that I believe will be very helpful to the readers of this book.

FOREWORD

At last, Kathy Labriola has given us the book we have needed for a very long time.

When I was a teenager, in the 1950s, divorce was a disaster that people whispered about. At that time, marriage was expected of everyone, and if your marriage had problems, you must be doing something very wrong.

The traditional concept of marriage in Western culture is based on the importance of family in agrarian society. Long-term commitments are needed to keep a farm going and ensure that nobody starves in the winter. Marriage meant stability, and stability was absolutely necessary for survival. This one-size-fits-all notion still shows up as our gold standard today, but the truth is that our financial security no longer depends on the stability of our relationships.

As we evolve into a new age of intimate partnerships, space opens up for each of us to enter into many different kinds of relationships, with many different kinds of people. Physical connections can be about many different kinds of sex, can include different genders, feature fantasies, or be about outercourse. Romance can be equally varied—from courtly to passionate, from "falling in love" to "I couldn't help it."

People live together for financial security, for companionship, as co-parents, retirement buddies, or nesting partners. Sex and romance may or may not be included in any one of these connections. We can achieve emotional security in any relationship by mutual support, transparency, and good communication. We can even enter into intimate connections out of curiosity, attracted by the appeal of something outside of our own culture and experience. For me, this was a revelation that allowed me to see outside the limits of my own family's values.

Let's not forget the magnetic attraction of opportunities to struggle with unfinished business from childhood. Many of us yearn to fix our parents, or to learn a better way to deal with bullies. Some relationships, even if brief, can provide a form of healing that helps us move through deeply rooted pain.

In any connection, there can be freedom of choice in how casual, deep, intimate, or autonomous you choose to be. It may not be your path to seek out abundance, but most people can expect to have at least several important relationships in a lifetime. Some of these relationships may be similar and a pattern may be revealed. Others may have wildly different relationship experiences.

Many of our relationships work best if they're allowed to run their natural course. For some, they can be considered as serving a purpose, and then when we have learned what we needed to, it's time to accept an end. Such connections might last weeks, months, or years, but duration is not the measure of their value.

With diversity in our love lives comes a lot more break-ups than in traditional relationship models, but this too is valuable experience. Consider what might change if we were to embrace the freedom of exploring sexual connections and relationships that may never become "the one." What would our lives be like if we valued each relationship for what is important in the connection, not for how close it comes to being the permanent pairing of our fantasies?

The old rules tell us that when a relationship doesn't work any more, someone must have done something wrong, that it must be someone's fault, that maybe we made a big mistake. The rules also insist that ending an intimate relationship must be drastically painful, terrifying, and enraging, that breakups always feature every scary emotion we can experience, at full volume.

We are told that the way to avoid feeling pain is to never set eyes on the person we were intimate with again, that it would be catastrophic and we couldn't bear it. So we make sure our friends don't invite the person we used to love to parties and social events. Only one of us may continue in that community, whether its a school, a job, or a neighborhood. There can be no more mutual friends.

But this reaction isn't necessary. Back in the 1970s, I spent about a year terribly depressed recovering from the breakup of a very special partnering. My ex, Robin, wanted to resume exploring our extra-special sexual connection, but I felt I couldn't. After my depression finally passed, we resumed our connection as intimate friends complete with our sexual dynamite and continued playing together for nine more years. It was definitely what we did best.

More recently, in 2015, my friends and family gathered around me while I underwent spinal surgery and a lengthy hospitalization. Joi, an ex of mine, took turns with my adult daughter sleeping in my hospital room for the first two weeks and offered endless support for months afterwards. I put out word that when I got out of the hospital, I could use a month in a guest room in San Francisco with no stairs and no need to drive. I was immediately offered healing sanctuary in the home of a dear friend with whom I broke up in 1979. Could it be that an army of exes cannot fail?

I'm terrifically grateful that my early years of refusing monogamy involved membership in a huge extended family of sluts, many of us with children, houses, careers, and all the other grown-up commitments. If I had a date with someone in that family, we'd start by hanging out at the home of whomever was hosting the children's pajama party so that the rest of us could go out dancing. When it was my turn to be with the kids, I got to co-parent 13 children and become auntie to quite a few more. The kids got abundant adult support and the experience of having siblings in a huge family plus the privilege of going home to a smaller family.

When a relationship within that family ended, we couldn't very well yank our children out of the family and tell them to shun their siblings, so we had to work things out in a way that didn't threaten the survival of our extended family. We wound up figuring out a lot of conflicts that I previously would have run away from and I learned a lot. One lesson was that the ending of an old relationship could be the beginning of a new one—often with the same person.

There's probably not much worse that you can experience with someone than breaking up with them. So, once you've recovered from the trauma of the breakup, old intimacy can fit as comfortably as an old glove. Perhaps sex is still a part, perhaps it isn't. Many of us have a fear that when someone gets to know us really, really deeply, they'll see a broken part of us that we are painfully ashamed of and work hard to hide. After a breakup, there's nothing hidden any more, and there's freedom in this.

So what could breaking up look like in this brave new world? Perhaps we could do a better job of it with a new set of skills. We were never taught to practise the art of breaking up and living to tell the tale, but maybe becoming skillful at breaking up might also serve you well in other conflicts in your life.

If you want to know what that might look like, you have the right book in your hands. Kathy Labriola uses her awe-inspiring repertoire of skills, wisdom, and experience to teach us that there isn't one, gold-standard way to do a "proper" breakup. She generously offers us choices to fit our various forms of relationships. She shows us how to find our way through uncharted briar patches, tells us where we might get lost and how we might find ourselves again, and teaches us how to stay conscious during the journey.

So step right up! By rethinking how you approach breakups, you can start building your personal support group of transcendentally comfortable old gloves today.

Dossie Easton
Marriage and Family Therapist
Co-author with Janet W. Hardy of *The Ethical Slut:
A Practical Guide to Polyamory, Open Relationships
and Other Freedoms in Sex and Love.*

INTRODUCTION:
UNDERSTANDING POLY BREAKUPS

As a counselor working with lots of people in all types of open relationships, I am acutely aware that not all poly relationships live happily ever after. In fact, most poly people go through a number of relationships, with some epic ups and downs, which often end badly. Most will eventually develop a strong relationship skill set, learn to pick appropriate partners, and figure out which model of open relationship works for them. Of course, some people never learn, and seem determined to indefinitely repeat the same mistakes. For most poly people, there is usually a steep learning curve that includes finding out the hard way how much time and energy they can devote to sex and relationships, and how many partners they can realistically juggle.

Meanwhile, it seems inevitable that there will be some extremely intense and painful breakups, which usually create more suffering than most people bargain for. Over the years, I have heard many people express shock and dismay at just how horribly painful these poly breakups turn out to be, and how long the healing process seems to take. The ending of any sexual or romantic relationship is bound to be painful, but a poly breakup creates its own unique set of challenges and complications.

This book is not a scientific study, and the data is primarily anecdotal. Because people seeking counseling are usually experiencing challenges and pain in their relationships, I was concerned that my sample might not be representative of open relationships in general. To get a broader view, I have done extensive interviews with poly people about their personal experiences of the dissolution of one or more polyamorous relationship(s). I interviewed 45 people from all over the US, as well as a few people in Europe and Asia, in order to get as wide a cross section as possible. Each interview was about three hours long, and I mercilessly interrogated each person about every aspect of their relationship from start to finish, as well as the aftermath of the breakup. While there are no hard statistics, there is a lot of information, and this book outlines my most-educated guesses based on the interviews and a few decades of counseling poly people through their breakups.

This book starts with a brief discussion of common assumptions about relationships and about breaking up, and explores how those beliefs affect our experience when a relationship ends. We are living in a society where monogamy is seen as the norm and marriage is supposed to last a lifetime, even though there is infidelity in the majority of marriages, and more than half of all marriages end in divorce. These somewhat unrealistic expectations also affect people in polyamorous relationships, and as a result, most poly people have some beliefs that may not be appropriate or useful in a polyamorous lifestyle.

The next part of the book is focused on the most common causes of poly breakups. About half of these relationships end due to causes that have nothing to do with the polyamorous nature of the relationship. Rather, they are caused by one (or more) of seven "garden variety" incompatibilities. These are the same reasons that people in monogamous relationships break up: sexual problems, incompatibility around money, domestic issues, conflicts over autonomy and intimacy, drug and alcohol addiction, untreated mental health conditions, and anger problems leading to verbal or physical abuse. This section also covers how pre-existing incompatibilities in one of these seven areas can be further intensified in an open relationship, as well as outlining some prevention strategies that can help sustain poly relationships.

The next section of the book tackles the other half of poly breakups, those in which some aspect of polyamory is the root cause of the breakup. Four key causes are addressed: a polyamorous person falling in love with a committed monogamist, picking partners who want a different model of open relationship than you do, poor management of time and energy, and, last but definitely not least, jealousy. Strategies for preventing these problems and reducing the risk of a relationship ending due to a polyamory-related cause are discussed.

The final section of the book provides coping strategies for surviving the ending of an open relationship. These include ways of taking care of yourself while grieving the loss of a relationship, sustaining any remaining relationships, learning what you can about yourself and relationships, and handling the reactions of friends and family members. The final two chapters discuss possibilities for increasing the likelihood of less painful breakups, the potential for transitioning from a romantic relationship to some form of friendship, and some thoughts about future relationships.

This book assumes a moderate amount of knowledge about open relationships. If someone is reading this book, they are probably already involved in a poly relationship or, sadly, have already experienced a poly breakup. Many existing books can provide an excellent tutorial on open relationships, including *The Ethical Slut, More Than Two,*

Stories From the Polycule, Opening Up, Polyamory in the 21st Century, and my previous books, *Love in Abundance* and *The Jealousy Workbook.*

BREAKUPS COME WITH THE (POLY) TERRITORY

A key difference between monogamous relationships and open relationships is the basic assumption that, in a poly relationship, not every new relationship can be expected to last a lifetime

Many people in open relationships make the mistake of believing that adding additional partners will be painless and permanent. The reality of living a poly life is that some partners will come and go over time, and when a new partner signs on to an open relationship, they are not promising to stay forever.

Various incarnations of poly relationships can end for a dizzying array of reasons. This is especially true for "casual" or "secondary" relationships, as both partners enter the relationship with a decreased level of commitment, and the changing needs of other relationships may doom these relationships at any point. For instance, a married or cohabitating couple may each have outside relationships, which may go on happily for years. However, if the couple has a baby or moves away because one of them takes a job or goes to grad school out of state, those outside relationships are likely to end or be drastically curtailed, no matter how healthy and satisfying they have been. Or if someone is in a casual relationship with someone unavailable for, or uninterested in, forming a more committed relationship, and they develop a primary relationship with someone else, they may decide to commit more fully to the primary partner and end any other relationships. And casual or secondary relationships often end because one partner is very unsatisfied with not getting enough time, attention, or priority from their partner. Or, as often happens, someone in a primary relationship decides to end that relationship because they find an open relationship too painful or complicated, and decide to seek out a monogamous relationship instead.

Another common reason for a relationship's demise is that poly people often take on additional partners quite quickly, without carefully vetting that partner for long-term compatibility. Of course monogamous people can also get wildly infatuated and sometimes jump into relationships without much forethought. However, because monogamous people are often looking for "the one and only," they are at least a little more likely to scrutinize any potential dating partner for common interests, similar values, emotional health, financial solvency, and good relationship skills. Many poly people reason that since they already have at least one other partner, the new relationship does not have to meet all of their relationship needs. Therefore they don't believe there has to be a high degree of compatibility, as their other partner or partners already provide a lot of love, sex, and companionship.

If the new partner has very different needs or has some basic relationship incompatibilities, the relationship is likely to end as soon as the sexual and romantic chemistry subsides. This does not have to be heartbreaking if both people recognize from the start that it is likely to be a delightful but short-lived love affair that does not have much potential to continue past the initial infatuation. However, in most cases, at least one of the people involved will become very emotionally attached to a future with that partner, and is likely to be crushed when reality proves that they have little in common. As a result, the success or failure of any specific poly relationship cannot be predicated on longevity. In fact, this can be reframed as an important strength of open relationships.

In a monogamous relationship, the beloved is expected to be the "soul mate" or life partner, so there is an assumption that the end of that love relationship means the relationship was a "failure." One of the liberating components of polyamory is being freed from these restrictive rules that encourage couples to stay together for life, or at least as long as they can stand it, despite how unhappy or mismatched they may be.

Most people have observed in their own families and communities that the vast majority of ostensibly monogamous people do not actually mate for life. In fact, most people who define themselves as monogamous actually practice one of the two relationship styles that are the predominant mating rituals of the early 21st century: serial monogamy, or professed monogamy with cheating.

Serial monogamy is practiced by many people of all sexual orientations. In this lifestyle, a couple is pair-bonded and sexually exclusive for some period of time, until they break up and move on to a new monogamous relationship, a pattern they repeat throughout their lives. It does not seem accurate to call these folks monogamous. While technically they have been sexually exclusive with each person for the duration of each relationship, many serially monogamous people have hundreds of sexual and romantic partners in their lifetime, so can they really be called monogamous? Many poly people have noted the irony of being considered promiscuous by their monogamous friends and relatives, when in fact many poly people have had sex with fewer partners than these same "monogamous" slut-shamers. For example, Georgia's monogamously identified friend said to her, "I don't understand how people like you can be poly and sleep around with all these people! I've been married for 15 years, and I am inherently monogamous, so I could never do that." When Georgia asked her friend how many people she had slept with in the past 25 years, she paused and eventually answered, "About 20 people." My client told her that during that same 25 years she had slept with a grand total of seven people, that three of these relationships happened concurrently, and that she is still with all three of those partners. So who is really "sleeping around"? As serial monogamy becomes much more typical, perhaps a new term should be invented that does not include the word "monogamy," as it hardly seems accurate as a description for people who have been sexually active with such a large number of people, even if it's only with one person at a time.

This has led some polyamorous people to ask, "Why are these serially monogamous people getting more action than we are? How is it that the monogamous people have more sex and more sex partners than we do?" That question is outside of the scope of this book, but I hope that some social scientist or scholar will thoroughly research this puzzling paradox.

Along with serial monogamy, "monogamy" with cheating is also very common. Numerous studies of married and cohabiting couples have come up with slightly different numbers, but all seem to agree that sexual infidelity occurs in over half of all married and cohabiting couples. People cheat on their partners for a hundred different reasons, but the end result is the same—they break their agreement to be monogamous and betray their partner's trust, usually repeatedly lying to them in the process.

Despite these contradictions, most "monogamous" people still believe in finding that one and only true love, and being together for life. As a result, they share the assumption that longevity is the true measure of a relationship's success. The myth of the one true soul mate remains potent, and while very few people actually remain sexually and romantically exclusive with one person for life, this entrenched belief apparently still trumps reality.

Many poly people seem to share the belief that a relationship's longevity is the only true yardstick of success. Because they bring this belief into their poly relationships, they are devastated when they discover that some poly relationships do not last forever. I often see clients who have just lost one of their lovers, and they feel shattered by insecurity, low self-esteem, and guilt. They vacillate wildly between blaming themselves, attacking their partner, doubting their sexual desirability, and wondering aloud whether they are even worthy of love. They fear meeting new people and are terrified of opening up to their hearts to trust anyone again, even their other pre-existing partners. Often the demise of the relationship had nothing to do with them, their relationship skills, or their attractiveness. Instead, the breakup may have been caused by circumstances completely out of their control. These could include the partner finding another lover who is more available for a committed relationship, being too busy raising kids, their partner's other partner vetoing the relationship, a decision to try being monogamous, the ramping up of job responsibilities, or moving to another state.

Poly people may find it useful to examine their core beliefs and develop their own criteria for healthy, happy relationships, where the longevity of each relationship is not the primary measure of success or failure. After all, how realistic (or even desirable) is it that every one of multiple relationships will last for the rest of your life? Think about other criteria based on the quality of the relationship and your quality of life in the relationship, rather than the quantity of time each relationship lasted.

For instance, did you have an intensely pleasurable and meaningful experience throughout that relationship? Was it a beautiful love that you will remember fondly all your life? Did you become a better lover or a better communicator through that relationship? Did you do a lot of exciting things together, such as taking great trips, seeing great concerts, or going backpacking and kayaking in the wilderness together? Did you learn new skills that you are grateful for, and that have improved your remaining relationships? Did you create something important together in that relationship, such as being in a band, performing in theater, or doing political activism together? Did you build a house or plant a garden together? Did you create children or take care of aging parents together? Aren't these experiences and achievements at least as important as whether the relationship lasted two years or 10 years or 30 years?

In Dr. Elisabeth Sheff's 2016 study of poly couples and families, she compares the worldviews of monogamous and polyamorous relationships: "Cultural norms define 'successful' relationships as monogamous and permanent in that the two people involved remain together at all costs. In this worldview, sexual fidelity is fundamental to the successful relationship and functions as both a cause and a symptom of relationship success. Polyamorists, in contrast, define the ends of their relationships in a number of ways in addition to success or failure. Polyamory is a form of non-monogamy in which people openly maintain (or wish to establish) multiple sexually and emotionally intimate relationships.

Poly people emphasize the importance of choice as a guiding principle for their lives and relationships. Focusing on the utility and health of their relationships, polys reported that if their relationships became intolerable, violated boundaries, or no longer met the participants' needs, then the correct response was to modify or end the relationship."

Adjusting expectations and curbing the fantasy of having multiple perfect and permanent relationships are likely to soften the blow when one or more partners moves on or proves incompatible. There doesn't have to be a villain or a victim. Transitioning from an erotic relationship to a platonic friendship, or "graceful distancing", is a lot more possible if the need to identify a guilty party and mete out blame and punishment can be circumvented.

PART ONE:
What Are the Most
Common Causes
of Poly Breakups?
And Can They
Be Prevented?

Poly vs. Non-Poly Causes of Breakups

No one seems to have any hard statistics on the many causes of poly breakups. My conclusions are based on decades spent counseling poly people about their breakups, as well as conducting extensive interviews specifically on poly breakups. Part One of this book covers the half of poly relationships that end due to causes other than polyamory. These relationships end for all the same reasons monogamous people break up, which I call The Usual Suspects or The Big Seven.

Many people are surprised to hear that at least half of all poly breakups have nothing to do with polyamory. The explanation for this is simple: Poly people are not any smarter about relationships than monogamous people and make the same unfortunate mistake of falling in love with people who are utterly incompatible with them. Some people have bragged that poly people are more highly evolved and are better at relationships than monogamous people, but that's not true. Unfortunately, when it comes to love and romance, poly people are just as likely to be completely delusional and have mush for brains as monogamous people. At least half of all poly breakups are caused by the same issues as monogamous breakups, but those same problems often have more complicated manifestations due to the non-monogamous nature of the relationship.

The Usual Suspects or The Big Seven

Many poly relationships and monogamous relationships end for the following seven reasons:

1. Sexual problems
2. Incompatibility around money
3. Domestic issues (conflicts arising from living together)
4. Conflicts over autonomy and intimacy
5. Drug and alcohol addiction
6. Untreated mental health conditions
7. Physical, verbal, or emotional abuse

CHAPTER ONE:

Sexual Problems Cause Lots of Monogamous Breakups and Lots of Poly Breakups

This includes basic incompatibilities around sex, such as differing libidos, different tastes in sexual activities, and power struggles around sex, as well as cheating and breaking agreements around sex.

Cheating is high on the list of sexual causes of break-ups. In a monogamous relationship, "cheating" usually means having sex and/or romance with anyone outside the relationship, and usually involves lying and a betrayal of trust. For monogamous couples, the definition of cheating seems to have been enlarged quite a bit in recent years to include emotional affairs. These are usually defined as close friendships that have some kind of romantic overtones, but which usually do not include sex or even explicit affection. They are seen as threatening to the monogamous pair-bond because so much intimacy and closeness is shared, and time is spent calling, texting, and emailing with that special person. A person having an emotional affair may deceive their spouse about the depth of the relationship.

Some of these emotional affairs are "cyber romances," often with someone who lives far away. The two participants may have never met in person, but carry on some type of fantasy relationship through email, sexting, and cyber sex.

Many other emotional affairs are with coworkers or are platonic friendships that gradually become more intimate and erotic, without actually crossing the line into becoming physical. Whether it involves a real life sexual relationship or an emotional affair, cheating in a monogamous relationship can, and often does, permanently destroy trust and safety, and can prove fatal to the relationship. Ironically, this is much more often due to the lying and sneaking around than to the affair itself. A surprising number of monogamous people say they could get over their spouse having sex with someone else, but cannot forgive the deception and "being played for a fool," because they feel they can never trust their partner after that. That their spouse was capable of lying to them about the affair often leads someone to wonder what else they may be lying about, and trust usually deteriorates from there. Many people are devastated that their partner broke such a core relationship agreement as monogamy, shaking their confidence in their partner's ability to keep any other agreements with them.

In poly relationships, many people also "cheat," but since sex with other people is allowed, cheating is usually defined as breaking an agreement about sex or other relationships. Some couples make agreements about sexual behaviors such as:

» Don't have unprotected sex with anyone but me.
» Don't sleep with my best friend or anyone in our immediate social circle.
» Don't have a relationship with any of your coworkers.
» Don't get any other women pregnant or don't get pregnant by any other man.
» Don't bring home any sexually transmitted infections and give them to me.

» Don't get so worn out from having sex with your other partners that you are too tired to have sex with me on the weekend.

» Don't have sex with anyone else in our bed.

» Don't fall in love with anyone you have sex with, just keep it casual or secondary.

» Don't have sex with someone new without telling me first (or full and quick disclosure reasonably soon after the fact).

Poly people may define breaking these agreements as cheating, and doing so may cause a poly breakup. As with monogamous people, many poly people say it is the broken trust, rather than the sexual behavior, that makes it hardest to get over a breach of one of these agreements. The logic is that if a partner had such bad judgment or cared so little about the agreements to disregard them and do whatever they want anyway, what is the point of making agreements? And what would prevent them from doing it again, or breaking any new agreements they make?

It's important to understand that any partner can make a mistake, especially if they are under the influence of lust, alcohol, drugs, or infatuation, despite their best intentions. I have seen poly people with the utmost integrity break an agreement around sex because an irresistibly compelling sexual or romantic opportunity suddenly presented itself, and they just felt unable to say no. Often, they say later that in the heat of the moment, they did not feel it would harm anyone, and that they somehow believed their spouse would understand and forgive them. However, once they see the terrible pain their actions have caused to someone they love, they are flooded with remorse, and are very likely to learn from that mistake and not repeat it.

For example, Vanessa and Juan attended Burning Man festival in the Nevada desert, and they had agreed it was fine to have sex with other people there, but to do so discreetly and not to bring anyone back to their shared camp. However, Vanessa was under the influence of Ecstasy when a lovely couple propositioned her for a threesome. She consented, and brought them back to the camp, thinking that since Juan had gone to a party at another camp it would be okay. She was also feeling too incapacitated by drugs to walk all the way to the couple's camp. Juan came home drunk from the party a little earlier than expected and walked in on the three of them having sex. A physical altercation ensued, which caused them all to be kicked out of Burning Man by security, and led to the demise of Vanessa and Juan's relationship.

In another example, Jon and Scott had recently gotten married, and had an agreement that it was fine to pick up guys at bars, sex clubs, or through dating apps like Grindr, but that it should be casual sex, a "fuck-buddy," or a friends with benefits arrangement. However, Jon met Warren on Grindr, and after having sex a few times they really clicked both sexually and emotionally, and developed a serious relationship. At first Jon was not completely honest with Scott about his feelings for Warren or how often he was seeing him. Instead, he told Scott that the relationship was casual, because he was afraid of hurting Scott or being forced to end the new relationship. When he did finally disclose the truth, Scott felt so betrayed by the dishonesty and threatened by Jon's attachment to this new relationship that he moved out and filed for divorce.

While sex and sexual issues can cause a lot of poly breakups, it should be mentioned that being poly can help *solve* some sexual problems. This is especially true of a so-called "desire discrepancy," which is just a fancy way of saying that one person wants sex more often than their partner. Having outside partners can certainly take the pressure off of a situation where you and your partner have mismatched libidos.

For monogamous couples, when one partner wants more sex than the other, they don't have the option of openly and honestly having other sex partners. As a result, their only available options are: to fight about sex constantly, for the lower-libido partner to go along with sex when they would rather not, for the higher-libido partner to be chronically sexually frustrated, for one partner to cheat, or to break up. Often all of the above options occur, usually in exactly that order, with the end result being the demise of the relationship due to sexual incompatibility.

Having multiple partners can allow each person can get their optimal amount of sex. However, this carries some risk, even for experienced poly couples. If you start having a lot of great sex with another partner because your partner at home has a lower sex drive than you do, you may start to transfer your romantic and sexual loyalty to the new partner, and start feeling a lot less intimate with your pre-existing partner.

This sometimes leads to ditching a long-standing relationship while in thrall of New Relationship Energy (NRE). People often mistakenly believe that the intense sexual chemistry and romantic infatuation in the new relationship means that they should abandon the more established relationship and run off into the sunset with the new paramour. This is usually a mistake, because comparing a long-term committed spouse with a passionate new lover is like comparing apples and oranges. A long-term relationship has a different set of costs and benefits than a hot new love affair. The pre-existing relationship cannot really compete with a new relationship for excitement and sparkle. This is partly because you don't really know the new lover well enough to see their faults or to have any idea whether you are really compatible for the long haul.

It's a good idea to think back to when you first got involved with your long-term partner, and remember that it was probably just as hot and passionate with them at the beginning and that the sizzle is bound to cool down eventually, usually sooner rather than later. I always advise people to wait until the infatuation subsides, or at least a year (whichever is longer), to decide whether there is a really good reason to choose a new relationship over one that has already proved it has a lot of staying power.

Lack of sex in a long-term relationship can also lead to a poly breakup for a different reason. In many cases, one partner has been unhappy about infrequent or non-existent sex in their relationship, but has been willing to accept it because they believed that their spouse simply has a low libido or lost interest in sex due to stress, fatigue, or some other extraneous reason. However, when that same person starts dating someone new and is obviously having sex outside the relationship, it becomes clear that they have actually not lost interest in sex, they have just lost interest in having sex with their pre-existing partner. What seemed tolerable when it appeared to be a generic lack of sexual appetite may now be unbearable. When your partner is having sex with someone else, it can feel like a very cruel sexual rejection and is often "the final insult" that causes the relationship to collapse.

For example, Peter and Susan were busy with their careers and two small children, so Peter was disappointed, but not so surprised, that their sex life had dropped off to nearly zilch for two years. When Susan started a hot new love affair with someone she met at a poly parents' support group, and was out having sex with him until 3 AM every

Friday night, Peter was crushed. He insisted that he and Susan revive their sexual relationship, saying that he felt displaced by this new man. "An outside relationship was not supposed to replace our sex life, it was just supposed to enhance our relationship. I didn't sign up for having a sexless marriage while you are out having sex with someone else!"

She responded that since they hadn't had much sex for years, why was he upset now, and why was he suddenly pressuring her for sex? She said she wasn't sure if she wanted sex with Peter anymore. Peter filed for divorce, saying that the sexual rejection had always been very painful, and he had tried to be understanding and let her set the pace for their sex life because he understood that she was tired and busy with the kids. But now that she was obviously sexually involved with someone else, he felt betrayed and humiliated, and like a chump for being so accepting of a very minimal sex life for the past few years.

This scenario is particularly common in lesbian relationships. Lesbian couples are much more likely than heterosexual couples or gay male couples to stop having sex altogether, or to have sex only rarely, perhaps a few times a year, after the first year or two of the relationship. Often the couple has a comfortable, emotionally intimate, and very affectionate relationship, so both women think that they are satisfied with the situation. Almost invariably, one of them eventually becomes sexually attracted to someone else and starts an outside sexual relationship. Suddenly the balance is disrupted, and the partner who is not having sex is devastated, since it is now clear that a non-sexual marriage was not so satisfying to her partner after all. It can be easier to accept no sex or very little sex when your partner says they are too tired, busy, stressed, or depressed to feel like having sex, or when they say "I just don't have much of a sex drive anymore." It is extremely painful to find that not only has your partner *not* wanted sex with you for years, but that they are eager to have sex with someone else. Sometimes the couple can revive their sexual relationship through couples' counseling, sex therapy, and resolving issues that may have been causing anger or distancing. However, much more often, this sexual change destroys the relationship.

The underlying question that must be answered by any couple in an essentially sexless relationship is this: Are sex, passion, and romance integral components of a committed relationship for you? Most people would say yes, that romantic and sexual connection is part of what defines a love relationship and separates it from platonic friendship. While many spouses are willing to accept some "dry spells" with no sex or very little sex in a long-term relationship, eventually they are likely to become dissatisfied without sex and end the relationship. This is true even for poly people who may have one or more partners outside of the relationship, because for most people, sex is part of the "glue" that makes them feel close to their partner, and they sorely miss the type of emotional intimacy that is usually facilitated by having sex with someone you love.

A good rule of thumb about whether polyamory will solve your sexual problems or lead to breaking up is whether you are actually having at least occasional and reasonably good sex with your long-term partner. Even if you are very frustrated by not getting enough sex in your relationship, but you are still having *some* sex and enjoying it, an outside sexual relationship is likely to help your relationship. This is because your goal is to outsource some of your sexual needs and supplement your existing sexual relationship with your partner, *not* to replace it. If you don't have satisfying sex with your partner, or if you are not having any sex at all with them, having great sex outside the relationship is only likely to reduce the emotional intimacy and closeness with your partner and create conflict and dissatisfaction in your relationship.

There are other sexual problems that polyamory can sometimes solve. For example, when one partner is kinky or BDSM-oriented and the other is either primarily "vanilla" or has only a small amount of interest in SM activities. Being able to pursue those kinkier activities with other partners can allow a person to satisfy more of their overall erotic and relationship needs, without pressuring their partner to participate in activities that do not appeal to them. And even if both members of a couple are very BDSM-oriented, they often have wildly divergent needs and desires. Being able to satisfy their core kinks with other partners can reduce conflict in the relationship and increase overall relationship satisfaction. However, if most (or all) of a person's BDSM needs are being met by another partner, they may begin to feel much more intimate with that partner and start to withdraw their love and investment from the pre-existing relationship. Because BDSM activities can be intense and create strong intimacy, bonding, and attachment, they may begin to feel that this other partner is better matched with their needs and desires, and feel less connected to their partner at home.

For instance, Aisha and Brenda, a cohabiting lesbian couple, were deeply in love and had a very emotionally intimate relationship. While they were very affectionate and spent a lot of time cuddling, their sex life was never very satisfying to either of them. It took them a few years to realize that they were both extremely submissive and craved being dominated sexually as well as in role-playing outside the bedroom. They joined the Exiles, a women's BDSM organization, and attended parties where they had a great time playing with dominant women, but nothing ever went beyond casual sex and role-play. Then Brenda went to an Exiles party while Aisha was out of town on business and met Bettina and Eve, who had the opposite problem. They were both doms, and as Eve put it, "Neither of us has a submissive bone in our bodies." They both topped Brenda at the party, and she rushed home to call Aisha to tell her they had won "the kinky lotto." She suggested that they pursue a "quad" or foursome relationship with Bettina and Eve.

While it sounded like a poly marriage made in heaven, after a few dates two things became painfully clear. Number one: Brenda and Bettina had fallen madly in love, or at least in lust and infatuation, and completely ignored their respective partners because they were hopelessly obsessed with each other. Number two: Aisha and Eve had no chemistry and actually found each other annoying, and both were terrified that their partners seemed to be abandoning them. Eve gave Bettina an ultimatum to stop seeing Brenda, but she refused, calling Eve "a controlling bitch." This precipitated a physical altercation on their front porch, with Eve grabbing Bettina by the arm and shouting, "Seriously? I'll show YOU some controlling, you skanky slut!" The neighbors called the police.

Bettina moved out and broke up with Eve, staying with her sister while continuing to pursue an intense relationship with Brenda. This made Aisha so jealous and insecure that she pleaded for constant reassurance that Brenda still loved her. They tried to have three-ways where Eve would top both of them, but Aisha felt excluded since there was such a strong bond between Eve and Brenda. Soon Brenda and Aisha were fighting so much that they decided to divorce. Within a month, Brenda had signed a lease on an apartment and Eve had moved in with her.

CHAPTER TWO:

Money Issues That Can Doom Both Monogamous and Open Relationships

Another key cause of breakups in both monogamous and polyamorous relationships is money. This includes a diverse group of issues, from having different values about making or spending money, to tensions about who is earning more money. There may be conflict about whether a partner is working hard enough or contributing enough financially to the household, different beliefs about how to manage money, when to be frugal and when to spend more freely, or tension due to being broke or in debt.

These issues are often further complicated when one partner is from a different social and economic class than their spouse, and they have been raised with very different financial realities. Ironically, not having enough money is the least likely money issue to doom a relationship. Lack of money will usually only lead to breaking up if each partner has very different beliefs about money and if they have differing approaches to solving their financial problems.

For most couples that break up due to money, it is because of different values and beliefs about money or different approaches to managing money.

Poly couples have all of the same problems and issues related to money that plague monogamous couples. However, in poly relationships, these problems usually have more complex and sometimes even more disastrous manifestations.

Often, pre-existing incompatibilities about money will be aggravated by a poly situation, and a financial issue related to polyamory will become the "last straw" that causes a break up. For instance, Jean and her wife, Penelope, had been fighting for years over their different approaches to their finances. However, their conflicts over outside lovers highlighted their differences in how they viewed work and money, and this proved to be the final nail in the coffin for their relationship. Jean worked full-time and made most of the money in the family. Penelope worked part-time because she was an aspiring sculptor, and wanted to spend most of her time making art. Jean had always had some resentment about her role as the primary breadwinner, while Penelope spent most of her wages on renting an art studio and buying expensive materials for sculpting. When Penelope started a new relationship, she cut her work hours even more, so she could spend time with her new girlfriend. Jean criticized Penelope for not contributing her fair share, and demanded she prioritize working more hours. Their arguments escalated until Jean insisted that Penelope break off the outside relationship. Penelope refused, and moved out.

Ongoing conflicts over one person working more hours or bringing more money into the household are often exacerbated by the arrival of a new lover. For Kevin, there was simmering discontent because he was the higher wage earner and already felt he was carrying too much of the financial load. Frankly, he felt his cohabiting partner, Jessie, was lazy and lacked ambition. He often criticized Jessie because she had an entry-level, part-time job that did not have much room for advancement. Kevin nagged her to work more hours or get a better-paying job. When Jessie added a new boyfriend to the mix, Kevin went ballistic. He felt financially exploited, angrily declaring, "While I'm out working long hours and bringing home a paycheck, instead of working, you're out having sex with some other guy!"

Jessie held her ground, reminding him that they had discussed their differing views on money many times over the years. Kevin acknowledged that he had always been willing, if grudgingly, to accept that she preferred to work fewer hours, be more frugal, spend less money, and have more free time for political activism and art. However, it felt very different to him that now she was making even less money, working fewer hours, and spending her free time having a relationship with another man.

"When you are volunteering at the local homeless shelter or going to City Council meetings, I feel good about working a little more to support that. But when you're out with Jim, I feel you are using me to support you financially, and being irresponsible," Kevin said. Jessie reminded him that while he made a lot more money, he also spent a lot more money than she did, eating lunch out every day, buying nice clothes, and driving a brand-new car while she rode a bike and got her clothes from thrift stores. "I have always supported your desire to spend your hard-earned money on expensive habits, since money is more important to you than it is to me. It's not fair to blame me for making less, since I only spend a fraction of the amount you spend every month," she said. This escalating conflict shone a spotlight on their glaring differences on financial matters, which caused Kevin to conclude that they were not compatible to be life partners, and he ended the relationship.

Money problems can arise in monogamous couples when partners decide to merge their money. Both people often put all their income and savings into "one big pot," and both dip into that pot for all their expenses. This often leads to fighting when one person spends too much money on things the other person believes are frivolous or has not agreed to. Perhaps one person wants to save as much as possible to buy a house or for retirement, and the other wants to give money to charities or political causes, buy gadgets, or go on expensive vacations.

Poly couples who merge their finances have exactly the same issues but with a particularly poly spin. For instance, your partner may be outraged that you are spending shared money on taking your new lover out for expensive dinners or buying gifts or flowers for your outside partners. Perhaps you spent a lot more money on Christmas gifts for your new boyfriend than you you did on gifts for your partner, and they can't help but notice because there it is on the Visa bill.

Or, conversely, your newer lover feels they are being treated unfairly because your pre-existing partner gets to share finances with you and make financial decisions together, but the two of you keep your finances separate. Or the newer partner feels restricted and controlled because you are not allowed to spend very much money on dates or other things you want to do together, because your other partner has a say in those decisions.

In one case, Karen got involved in a relationship with Kim, who was living with Beth. Kim and Karen wanted to go away for the weekend to celebrate their one-year anniversary of dating, but Beth would not allow Kim to spend any of their joint money on such a trip. Karen offered to pay all the expenses for the trip herself, with no contribution from Kim, and Beth agreed to this. However, Karen became very resentful that she could only go away with Kim if she paid for everything, and felt this was very unfair.

Kim, Beth, and Karen had a mediation session and came up with a compromise that worked for everyone. Kim was a nurse who often worked overtime, and she received overtime pay for those hours. With the help of the mediator, they decided that when Kim got any overtime pay, she could put that money aside to use for trips and other expenses in her relationship with Karen.

So financial issues are usually already a sticking point in a relationship, but adding a poly relationship only underlines a problem and makes it intolerable. Many poly couples at least partially solve this problem by separating their finances, having individual checking accounts and credit cards, etc. This way, each person can manage their own money and each pay their half of the mutual bills, while having the freedom to treat their other lovers to lunch or go to a concert with them without their spouse saying, "I'm pissed off that you're using *our* money to pay for dates with your other girlfriend," or "How come you paid $200 to go to the spa to get massages together and you never take me anywhere romantic like that?"

Conflict over who will care for children can also create money-related problems. This usually happens when one person quits their paying job after giving birth, or one person drops out of the paid labor force to provide childcare for their biological kids and/or other children in the poly family. While this is a financial issue, it will also be discussed in the next section because it is also a domestic issue. But because values about money and work are the core issues, it is being discussed here as well.

Often, poly families do not talk through the financial ramifications, or the work required, in raising children. They may not clarify who will pay these costs and who will do the work. Unfortunately, many poly people fail to make agreements in advance of the birth of a child. And many times, a partner who already has children moves in with other partners without discussing whether the other partners will financially support and physically provide care for those children. As a result, different assumptions are made by everyone involved, and disaster usually ensues, often leading to breaking up.

For instance, will each partner spend some of their time caring for all the children in the household, and will all partners share in the cost of professional childcare? If so, how many hours a day, or how many days of the week? Will each partner be expected to participate equally in child-rearing, or will the biological parent or parents have sole responsibility or more responsibility? Who will provide financial support for the children, and how much?

Sometimes, the biological mother (and in some cases, the bio-dad) assumes she will stay home with the baby and be supported financially by the rest of the family, while other members may have not agreed to this or even discussed it. More often, a poly family agrees in advance to provide financial support for the bio-mom to stay home and take care of the baby for a specific length of time, usually six months or one year, but then the parent extends that time. The rest of the family may feel betrayed because they never consented to this.

Sometimes, family members agree in advance to provide financial support for the parent(s) and the baby, but then find that they really resent paying for someone else's expenses, begin to feel it is unfair to them, and demand to change the agreement.

The child or children may be at a childcare center all day because all members of the household are working, and the biological parent or parents assume that all partners will share equally in the cost. In one V triad poly family with a man and two heterosexual women, the new mom had the family's agreement to hire a childcare professional to take care of the baby full-time in their home. The new mom failed to mention that she was planning to pay the childcare worker's salary out of the house checking account. She assumed this was a household expense, but her partner's other partner said, "Why should I pay for childcare for your baby? I didn't get you pregnant, and it's not my responsibility."

An unplanned pregnancy is even more likely to lead to the demise of a poly relationship, often because suddenly each partner is being forced into a situation they never agreed to, and the other partners have very little control over whether the biological parent(s) will choose to have the baby or terminate the pregnancy. Sometimes having family counseling can help a poly family find some way of resolving this situation. The pregnant partner may decide to end the pregnancy if it becomes clear that one or more partners does not want to become a parent and will leave the relationship over this. Or the other partners may realize how important continuing the pregnancy is to their partner, and become more accepting and welcoming of the new baby.

Some poly partners may not want responsibility for supporting a child financially, especially if they had no involvement in creating the pregnancy, and no control over the decision to continue it. They may not agree to provide financial support for one or more parents to stay home with the baby and feel resentment over these expectations. Sometimes counseling or mediation can help a family find compromises that make everyone feel respected and comfortable. However, many unplanned pregnancies lead to divorce or the breakup of poly families due to irreconcilable differences.

CHAPTER THREE:

Domestic Issues That Can Lead To Breakups

Problems described as "domestic issues" also doom many relationships, both poly and monogamous.

Domestic issues include all the tensions that can arise from two or more people living together. These include conflict centered around housework, cleanliness, scheduling activities, deciding whether to have children, how to raise kids, policies about guests, how to deal with in-laws and other relatives, roommates, noise, food preferences, cooking, and the division of labor in the household. In poly relationships, as with sexual issues and money problems, domestic issues are often already causing conflict, and then the poly situation amplifies the tension and eventually causes a breakup.

Many poly relationships start out with a heterosexual couple, where the wife is already unhappy because the man is not doing his share of housework and childcare.

For example, an unequal division of labor was already a serious cause of fighting in Marcia and Joe's marriage long before they decided to open up their marriage to other partners. Marcia was already dissatisfied and pleading with Joe to do more of the domestic work. When they then became polyamorous and he was out on dates with Gail a few nights a week, she was outraged and filed for divorce. Joe was baffled about why Marcia had such an "extreme reaction."

At a couples' counseling session Joe explained that on the nights when he was at home, he was sitting on the couch drinking beer and watching TV, while Marcia cooked dinner, washed the dishes, and put the kids to bed. So as he put it, "I'm not doing any work when I'm at home, so what's the difference if I'm out seeing my girlfriend? Either way, you're doing the same amount of work." Marcia explained that she was always angry that he was not doing anything to help, but that his being out on dates with the new girlfriend added insult to injury. "When I'm home all alone with a sick kid, and cleaning up barf and changing diapers, knowing that you are out having sex with another woman makes me want to murder you," she said.

This story actually has a happy ending, because Joe's new lover, Gail, made a simple but brilliant suggestion. Joe could continue to go out with Gail two nights a week. One other night of the week he could watch TV and drink beer, and have no chores at home. Three other nights of the week, he would help Marcia with the cooking and also do a load of laundry, which he could fold while watching TV after dinner. On the one remaining night of the week, Marcia could take a long hot bath with a glass of wine, while Joe cooked dinner on his own and washed the dishes, then she would put the kids to bed. After a month of trying this out, Marcia said, "Gail is a genius, I am really starting to like her."

In situations where a poly triad or foursome lives together, domestic issues frequently cause breakups. Many people have discovered, to their dismay, that it's hard enough to live with one partner and achieve some amount of compatibility around housework, whether to eat meat or not, whether you can smoke pot in the house, childrearing practices, clutter, noise levels, enjoying the same social activities, etc. So what are the odds that three or four people will have such a high-level of affinity that they can live together harmoniously? Sex and relationship advice columnist Dan Savage has said, "I've been to several poly families' commitment celebrations, but I've never been to a poly family's third anniversary celebration." While he later admitted that this was "kind of an asshole thing to say," there is a kernel of truth to his words, as only a small fraction of poly threesomes and moresomes actually survive living together for more than a year or so.

The more you are informed about the challenges and potential pitfalls of your relationships, the more accurately you can assess the viability of cohabitation for you and your partners. Then, if you decide to go forward with living together as a poly family, you can take steps to maximize your chances for success.

There are three key ingredients for making it work:

1. Compatibility among all partners on most aspects of living together.
2. A high degree of flexibility and willingness to compromise and accommodate the needs of all family members.
3. Excellent interpersonal skills, good communication, and healthy boundaries.

These ingredients are crucial in *any* polyamorous relationship, but are absolute necessities if you are all living together.

There has to be a lot of agreement on everything, including where to live, whether to buy or rent a house or apartment, how clean to keep the house, who will be responsible for which chores, what kind of food to buy and who will cook meals, how much privacy or personal time each partner and each relationship will have, and how much time will be spent together as a family. This turns out to be a pretty high bar to meet, and the majority of poly living groups find it very challenging, if not impossible.

The more people in the household, the more complicated it is for everyone to have enough room and control over their space, and the harder it is to get the right balance of togetherness, alone time, and privacy.

It often works better for everyone in a poly family to move into a new, neutral space that no one is already emotionally attached to. This way everyone is starting off fresh, with the same amount of power and investment in creating a home that works for everyone.

Some poly triads and a few poly quads have solved some of these dilemmas through the creative use of architecture. They have done this by living in a duplex or a house with a cottage in the backyard, or even two apartments in the same complex. These arrangements means that everyone can spend a lot of time together, but they don't have to be as compatible as would be required to live together in a single space.

Mildred, who was part of a successful long-term poly family that bought a duplex together, says, "Financially, it's an expensive solution. However, it's still much cheaper than divorce, because if we got divorced we'd have to rent two apartments, anyway. And this is much better for our kids, they have all the parents, and all their stuff, in one place and they can easily go back and forth any time by just opening a door."

Jolene, another self-described "poly veteran" in a group marriage, found a similar solution. "Sharing a bed and sharing bodily fluids with three other people turned out to be much easier than sharing a kitchen and bathroom with them," she says. "Why? Because two of them are guys! Norm and Rob don't mind piles of dirty dishes in the sink, and they don't even notice the moldy wet towels in the bathroom and layers of soap scum in the bathtub. Raven and I were totally grossed out and we were constantly cleaning up after them. We were on the verge of moving out and getting our own place. It turned out it was cheaper to convert our two-car garage into an extra kitchen and bathroom. Norm and Rob agreed to use that bathroom, and to wash all their dirty dishes in that kitchen. So now Raven and I can keep our bathroom and kitchen clean, and we don't care how dirty theirs are, we just keep the door closed and don't think about it."

In another example, two middle-aged married couples became a poly quad, which evolved slowly over a period of years. Both of the women, Rosa and Natalie, were bisexual, and they developed a relationship first, while the men, Marvin and Robert, were platonic friends and the four of them socialized a lot together. After two years of being lovers, Rosa developed a crush Natalie's husband, Marvin. With Natalie's encouragement, they became lovers, and eventually Natalie and Robert developed an enjoyable sexual relationship as well.

They decided to live together as a group in Marvin and Natalie's large three-story Victorian house in San Francisco, since their children were grown and the three upstairs bedrooms were empty. However, it turned out that moving in together made it difficult for each individual relationship to get enough time and privacy, as they were all together in the house and had a very difficult time negotiating private time for each couple.

Natalie and Rosa would try to have a date night, but the men would always want to come along, and feel left out if they were not included. Rosa and Robert wanted to spend time alone together a few nights a week, as they had done for 25 years in their own home, but Marvin felt they were being rude and withdrawn if they wanted to have dinner separately. And with so many people involved, it seemed difficult for Marvin to ever get on Rosa's calendar for an individual date, and he began to feel she was rejecting him as a lover.

The entire poly family was on the verge of divorce when they realized that all of the four relationships could survive if they did not all live together. They were able to remodel the house and to make the upstairs a separate apartment with a kitchen. The apartment had an existing full bathroom, two bedrooms, and an office, and Rosa and Robert were already living in that part of the house anyway. The four of them decided that each weekend they would make plans a week ahead, so everyone could have dates with each of their respective lovers each week. They would have dinner together as a foursome a few nights a week, as well as doing other projects, and yard work together on weekends.

Shelley and Ricardo are a married couple from Boston who met and courted Mike and Chandra, a couple from New York. Two years after meeting, Mike and Chandra moved in with Shelley and Ricardo in Boston. However, the living situation was cramped and they all realized that they were not ready to give up their privacy, nor were they willing to share their finances. Mike and Chandra considered moving back to New York.

Shelley and Ricardo had a small house on a large lot, so they agreed to sell half the lot to Mike and Chandra, who built a small house for themselves on their half. The two couples now spend most of their time together. Some nights they all sleep together in one room. Other nights they make dates with individual partners so that each relationship can have more privacy. Each couple or any individual can withdraw to their own house if they want time alone or to pursue their own projects.

Bill and Esther had been married for six years when Bill met Rachel and developed a committed relationship with her. With Esther's consent, Bill began dividing his time equally between their home and Rachel's home. Rachel had never had children, and at age 40, wanted to have a child with Bill. Esther had 21-year-old twins from her previous marriage, who were both in college, and she did not want to start over with a new baby. They solved this dilemma by moving into a co-housing community where Bill and Esther could have their own cottage on the same property as Bill and Rachel's house. This way they could all have dinner together every night and spend most of their time together, but have two separate households. Bill continued to spend half of each week living with each partner, and he and Rachel had a baby together.

For years, Carmen was torn apart by the escalating demands of her lovers, Tanya and Katy. Katy had actually broken up with Carmen, who became so despondent that Tanya called her and "coaxed her back into the fold" with what turned out to be a great idea. The three women have now owned a duplex together for 10 years. Carmen spends three nights each week upstairs with Tanya, and three nights downstairs with Katy. The seventh day of the week is "Carmen's time," and she can negotiate to spend time with either woman if they are available, or to have time to herself. Tanya and Katy each have outside romantic relationships, and they see their other girlfriends when Carmen is with the other partner.

There seems to be a built-in occupational hazard when two couples get together. Many poly households start with a primary couple who add another couple, but then eventually end up as a threesome. It seems quite rare that all four people are compatible and flexible enough to handle the demands of a poly family, and eventually one of the four people opts out. There are also some group marriages where two or even three of the partners stay together for many years but the fourth or fifth partner leaves and is replaced every few years.

For instance, Denise, Millie, and Joseph have lived together for 10 years as a family. Millie and Joseph's two children also live with them. Denise was married to Bob and Millie to Joseph. The two couples met over the internet and courted, and eventually all moved in together as a poly family. Many conflicts developed because Bob was unhappy with the behavior of Millie and Joseph's children. There were also disagreements over finances, including how money was spent. Eventually Bob moved out and he and Denise divorced. Denise grieved losing her marriage with Bob, but continued living with Millie, Joseph, and the children. She now says, "We seem to be living happily ever after." Millie identifies as the primary parent and works full-time at home, taking care of the children, house, and garden. Denise and Joseph both work full-time outside of the home, and are happy to support Millie financially. Denise says, "It's so wonderful to come home from work every night to a clean house, dinner on the table, and a beautiful, smiling wife greeting me with a kiss at the door! Every woman should have a wife!"

In many poly families, conflicts center on how much responsibility the partners feel is appropriate to take on for each partner's extended family. One poly foursome broke up when a woman's 30-year-old daughter and her two small kids suddenly moved in with them after a messy divorce. The mother expected her poly family to provide free accommodation, food, and childcare for her daughter and grandchildren. The family refused, and she and one of the other partners moved out.

Another family fell apart when one man's elderly father developed Alzheimer's and needed full-time care and supervision. The man wanted his father to move in and be financially supported and physically cared for by his poly family members. His partners felt this was not realistic since each partner had a full-time job and no one could stay home to care for his father.

In both families, these situations were never predicted or discussed in advance. In each case, one partner believed it was their poly family's responsibility to care for their biological family members in need, but their poly partners had not agreed to this, and refused to do so.

When poly partners meet and fall in love, they are generally focused on romance and the excitement of creating a family together. They usually aren't thinking about worst-case scenarios in the future. As unpleasant as it may seem to talk about potential problems, it's wise for poly families to clarify expectations of each partner and discuss how such situations will be handled before they move in together. This way all partners have a say in these decisions and there will be consensus on what to do in the event of illness, disability, job loss, divorce, or other big changes.

As touched on in the discussion of financial issues, incompatibility around children and childrearing has doomed many poly relationships. A lot of poly families are "blended" families with one or more children from previous relationships. This often creates conflicts over scheduling custody arrangements with ex-spouses, as well as negotiating complex childcare agreements for poly family members. Sometimes the biological parent(s) object strongly to other partners providing limits or discipline for their children. There can be sharp disagreements among multiple partners over children's behavior, bedtimes, homework, activities, or diet, and it can be impossible to reach consensus.

Disputes over childcare sometimes break down along gender lines: The women in the household often do way more than their share of the parenting and struggle to convince the men to pull their weight. In two of the poly families who agreed to be interviewed, the women left the families and took the children with them because they felt so unsupported by their male partners in child-rearing duties.

If there are no children when the poly family is initially formed, irreconcilable differences may develop if one partner wants children and others don't. Many poly families have disbanded because one partner wanted children but could not persuade the others to agree. An all-too-common scenario is a Female-Male-Female triad where the pre-existing heterosexual couple already has children, and the newer woman in the triad wants to have a child. Often, the couple does not want to raise any more children, which sometimes causes the newer partner to end the relationship.

Jose and Jillian were a cohabiting couple who fell in love with Nancy, and the three became lovers. Nancy already had a four-year-old daughter, Tiffany, and they spent a lot of time together as a family. Then Nancy accidentally became pregnant by Jose, and Jose and Jillian asked her to move in with them so they could raise the baby together. Living together through the pregnancy proved rocky, as Jillian was resentful of both the attention Nancy was receiving, and that Nancy seemed to expect her to take care of Tiffany all the time since the pregnancy was making Nancy very tired. Jillian was doing all the housework and cooking, as well as working full-time. Jose worked long hours, and was only able to help with childcare and household chores on weekends. After the baby was born, Jillian became even more resentful as she felt Nancy wanted to be waited on all the time and was ignoring Tiffany because of the new baby. Tantrums ensued, both from Tiffany and from Jillian.

In all the excitement about the pregnancy, they had failed to talk through how the childrearing and the division of labor would work. And although all three of them had agreed that Nancy would stay home with the baby for six months, Jose and Jillian did not realize that Nancy did not have any money saved, and that she was expecting them to support her, Tiffany, and the new baby, Tyrone, for that whole time. They begrudgingly paid all the bills, but after six months Nancy refused to go back to work, insisting on staying home for another year. Jillian and Jose were tired of supporting Nancy and the children financially, and were angry that Nancy was breaking her agreement. They insisted that Nancy go back to work or move out. She had no choice but to concede, and returned to her job. However, she refused to pay any bills, putting her entire paycheck in the bank. As soon as she had saved up enough money, she rented an apartment and moved out. She initiated a custody battle to prevent Jose from having any custody of his son and asked for child support.

But not every situation is disastrous. For the poly families who find a way to live together happily, the rewards are great: lots of companionship, stable romantic and sexual relationships, a built-in social life and community, more adults to share housework, multiple incomes to achieve a more comfortable standard of living and long-term financial security, an economy of scale that lowers living costs, the option of sharing resources, and additional adults to care for children, ill or disabled family members, and elders.

CHAPTER FOUR:

Incompatible Needs for Intimacy and Autonomy

In any relationship, there will be some conflict over the regulation of intimacy and autonomy, but it manifests with a different set of problems in polyamorous relationships than in monogamous couples.

No two people are perfectly matched in their respective needs for closeness as a couple and their need for time alone and privacy. This spectrum can be conceptualized as a scale of zero to 10. There is a broad range, with complete independence at the zero end of the scale, and 24/7 "joined-at-the-hip coupledom" at the other upper end. Each person has an ideal comfort zone that feels right to them for how much personal privacy, autonomy, and control over their own life they need, and how much love, intimacy, togetherness, and merging they want with a partner. One person in any given couple will always want more independence and more of a life of their own, and the other will always want more integration of their lives.

Anyone who is between a two and an eight on the scale can probably have a healthy and happy relationship.

Anyone who is below a two will have difficulty maintaining a relationship, because they are not willing or able to give a partner enough time, attention, and intimacy to keep them satisfied. People who are above an eight will also find it difficult to sustain relationships, because their demands for time, attention, and loyalty would make most people feel smothered. Anyone between a two and an eight can probably find partners who want a similar balance between having a life of their own and being in a committed relationship, as long as they pick partners who are relatively close to their number on the autonomy/intimacy scale.

For monogamous couples, discrepancies in these needs often prove fatal to the relationship, since they are not allowed to meet any of their needs for love and intimacy outside of their primary relationship. If they are too far apart on the scale, they will be forever locked in a power struggle. One will fight to maintain independence and control, carving out private time and space, and the other will experience a chronic scarcity of time, attention, affection, and closeness.

One person eventually flees due to the escalating demands for intimacy, or the other feels so starved for love and affection that they end the relationship. Some monogamous people try to solve this problem by seeking emotional intimacy and connection from close friends or family members, but often the "missing ingredients" are affection, romance, and sex, which are off-limits for monogamous people outside of their relationship. Unfortunately, this usually leads to a partner cheating.

Sometimes, one partner's need for more closeness and romantic attention drives monogamous couples to try poly-amory. However, this can sometimes lead to the demise of their relationship. This is because they are not truly polyamorous people, but are only trying an open relationship as a problem solving strategy. The danger is that the partner who goes outside the relationship for intimacy is likely to choose someone who is more closely matched to their intimacy needs, and may decide to leave the primary relationship for a monogamous relationship with the new partner.

Couples who are considering polyamory should think carefully about whether it could potentially jeopardize their relationship. If you actually want a monogamous relationship, but are simply incompatible with this particular partner, polyamory is not the answer.

But open relationships can solve *some* of the problems created by different autonomy/intimacy needs within a couple. Either partner can have additional relationships if they experience a scarcity of time and attention in their primary relationship. In addition, if a partner is feeling overwhelmed by their partner's demands for togetherness, they can encourage their partner to seek outside partners to take the pressure off them.

However, this can lead to some interesting *new* problems. For instance, Sandra was an eight on the autonomy/intimacy scale, and her partner, Steve, was a three. Sandra spent years feeling lonely, rejected, and unloved because Steve, a biochemist, spent a lot of weekends working on research in his lab, and when at home he wanted to spend a lot of time reading scientific articles and watching movies. Sandra got involved in two secondary relationships with other men, but she was spending so much time on these two new romances that Steve began to complain of being neglected. The demands of her two new lovers felt overwhelming, and she eventually felt compelled to cut back.

A more difficult problem can be created if the person who is at the lower end of the intimacy/autonomy scale chooses to enter into outside relationships. For instance, John is a two and Alice is a six. Alice is generally satisfied because she has an outside relationship to satisfy her intimacy needs. Then, someone makes a pass at John and he decides to go for it, and Alice responds with panic. She knows that John has a low tolerance for intimacy and not much time and energy to devote to relationships. As a result, if he has another partner, Alice is likely to receive even less attention. She wants him to abandon the other relationship and reserve his relationship energy for her, since there is a shortage already. His need for a lot of privacy and alone time will make it very difficult for him to sustain two relationships.

John may only discover what his limits are by trying to maintain two relationships and finding out the hard way that he can't manage it. He may find that a casual outside sex partner or a long-distance relationship would work fine. If he goes forward in pursuing an intense relationship, he probably won't give enough time and attention to Alice. If the amount of romantic love and attention then drops below the current minimum amount, she is likely to end the relationship.

Prevention Strategies

If you are in an open relationship, it is advisable to think carefully about where you are on the autonomy/intimacy scale, and to consider how this may affect your relationships. How much time and energy can you reliably devote to intimate relationships? How much intimacy and connection do you need? How much privacy and independence do you need for your life to feel satisfying and balanced?

In past relationships, did you often feel a need for more closeness, and feel frustrated and lonely because you did not get enough time and attention from your partner? If so, you are probably a six, seven, or eight on the scale. Seek partners who are also a five or above on the scale, who are likely to want a similar amount of attention and connection. However, you can get in a lot of trouble by picking partners who, like yourself, are "high maintenance." You will be besieged by their demands, and it is unlikely that you will be able to keep multiple partners happy.

A good rule of thumb for poly people is to pick at least one partner who is a few numbers lower than they are on the scale. For instance, it works well for an eight to pick a seven or eight as a primary partner as long as any additional partners are below a six. This configuration works because you can reserve enough time and energy for your primary partner and still have enough left over for an additional partner.

Conversely, if you are usually the person trying to keep your partners from taking up too much space in your life, you are probably a two, three, or four on the scale. You would be smart to pick a primary partner who is also between two and four, who highly values their independence, wants to have a lot of alone time, and have a life of their own. Some people who are a two, three, or four find that it works best to limit their outside relationships to very casual play partners, to go to sex parties for one-time sexual partners, or to choose other forms of "low-maintenance" outside relationships.

Some people who are at the lower end of the scale decide they do not want to have primary relationships at all, and do better having two or more non-primary relationships, where there is not such a big demand for intimacy and togetherness. For some people this is the ideal lifestyle and satisfies their needs for romance, sex, love, and companionship without the pressures of constant interaction and intimacy.

CHAPTER FIVE:

Problems One Partner Brings into the Relationship, Including Addictions, Untreated Mental Health Conditions, and Abuse

Some relationships end because of problems that were not created within the relationship. These include addictive behaviors, as well as untreated mental health conditions, and abuse.

These issues cannot really be called relationship problems, because they did not originate in the relationship. Instead, one person brought the problem with them and only they can solve it. If one person in the relationship has a cocaine addiction, for instance, only that person can fix that addiction, by getting the help they need to stay clean and sober. Or, if one person has an untreated mental health condition such as depression, anxiety, or borderline personality disorder, only that person can address it. If a partner has problems with anger management, only they can resolve that with counseling, anger management classes, or by finding some other way to address the root causes of their anger. In these situations, their partners are powerless to solve the problem, no matter how much they may try. However, these problems will inevitably cause the demise of relationships if the partner who has the problem does not take action or get help.

Addiction

Addiction is a heartbreaking problem that destroys many relationships, both monogamous and polyamorous. However, in poly relationships, addiction often plays a more complicated role in a breakup. In a poly relationship, an addict is often able to hide their addiction for much longer, especially in a secondary or casual relationship where they may not spend as much time with any one partner as they would in a monogamous relationship.

Krista explained, "I have a wife who I live with, and I was only seeing Jeffrey once every couple of weeks or some-times once a month, so it didn't seem odd that he liked to drink a couple bottles of wine and smoke some pot on every date. We liked to go out dancing, and he was that really fun party boyfriend. It wasn't until he totaled his car and nearly killed us on the way home from a club, then spent the night in jail because he was driving drunk, that I realized he had a problem. Of course I should have seen the warning signs sooner. But we always had a great time together, and I wasn't looking for a serious relationship with him, so I wasn't really scrutinizing him or his drinking."

When someone is not living with a partner, they can behave normally on dates but then go home and drink themselves into a stupor, or stay up all night taking speed. Usually, it takes a lot longer for a partner to notice all the signs of drug or alcohol addiction in a polyamorous rela-tionship than in a monogamous one. A poly partner may only realize they are in love with an addict when there are really obvious consequences such as getting fired from a job, health problems, legal problems such as DUIs, or strained relationships with family members and friends.

And sometimes substance abuse or drinking is already a problem in a primary relationship, but has not spiraled out of control until a poly relationship adds more stress to an already unhealthy situation. For instance, Sheila had a drinking problem throughout her 10-year marriage to Doug. She drank every night at home, and got giggly and incoherent while they hung out on the couch talking or watching TV. Doug tried to persuade her to moderate her drinking, without success. Then, they opened up their marriage and Doug developed an outside relationship. When he was out on dates with Jenny, Sheila would get drunk and call him on the phone screaming obscenities. A few times she got in the car drunk and drove to Jenny's house. Neighbors called the cops because she was banging on the door yelling. Each time, she would not even remember her behavior the next morning. Doug begged her to go into treatment to get sober, but she refused, claiming that his new relationship was the cause of her drinking. He agreed to stop seeing Jenny, but even then, Sheila would not stop drinking or get help. Doug and Sheila divorced.

What About Sex Addiction?

Many poly relationships end because one partner is using polyamory as a cover for compulsive and destructive relationship patterns. Just as some people choose monogamy for unhealthy reasons, some people choose polyamory to act out addictive behaviors in sex and relationships.

Polyamorous people bristle at being called sex and love addicts, because so many people erroneously believe that only sex addicts concurrently have more than one sexual or romantic partner. There are many happy, healthy, poly people, but there are also many sex and relationship addicts masquerading as polyamorists. People who have an addictive relationship with sex or love make very poor relationship partners, because they are too self-centered and too caught up in their own disease to be capable of real intimacy or love. Getting involved in a poly relationship with a sex or love addict is highly likely to cause heartbreak and, eventually, the demise of the relationship.

Sex addicts feel compelled to engage in frequent sexual activity with many partners, regardless of the consequences. The need for more sex and more partners clouds their judgment, and they often violate their own values and break existing agreements with partners. They use sex similarly to how other addicts use drugs or alcohol: to experience an intense high they can't get any other way, or to numb loneliness and emotional pain

Conversely, love and relationship addicts are excessively dependent on being in love and being in a relationship. They organize their lives around their relationships and sacrifice their own needs, their careers, and even their own self-respect in order to stay in relationships no matter how badly they are treated

Healthy poly people prioritize sex and intimate relationships in their lives and usually spend more time and energy than the average person sustaining their relationships. The key differences between polyamory and sex or relationship addiction are the addicts' lack of control over their behavior, and their inability to make rational choices about sex and relationships.

Many poly breakups are caused by one partner's sex or love addiction. For example, Alan is a heterosexual man who is a sex addict. He has been married and divorced twice, both times to poly women. In his first marriage, he made unwelcomed sexual advances to every one of his wife's female friends, and she eventually lost all of her friends because they got tired of being sexually harassed by him. His second marriage ended because he got fired for making unwelcome sexual overtures to coworkers.

Lisa is a bisexual woman who is polyamorous. She likes to go to sex parties, but makes poor partner choices and goes home with questionable, and even dangerous, men. Her husband left her because she had unprotected sex with a stranger and accidentally became pregnant.

John is a recently divorced gay man who is a love addict. His husband left him after becoming fed up with his addictive relationships. John had a long series of brief but intense outside relationships with other men. In each case, after a few months, he would lose interest and fall for someone new.

Prevention Strategies

Learn to recognize the symptoms of addiction, particularly when considering a potential partner. This is harder than it seems, since people often hide their addictive behaviors, or avoid indulging in them at the beginning of a new relationship. And since many people enjoy social drinking and recreational drugs it can be difficult to tell when someone has developed an addictive relationship with drugs or alcohol. Because poly people often have active and intense sex lives, sex addiction can be even more difficult to assess.

Sometimes there will be obvious red flags, such as losing a job due to coming to work hungover, or even being under the influence of drugs or alcohol at work. Not keeping agreements about safer sex, having poor boundaries with other partners, or picking inappropriate partners may indicate a sex or love addiction. However, there are often more subtle clues like a partner always being broke despite having a good job. You may eventually discover that the money is being used to pay for drugs. Vague health problems such as always having headaches and fatigue, or constant stomach problems with no explanation may be a sign of alcohol abuse. Or you may hear about unexplained legal problems requiring a lot of court appearances and lawyer fees. Most often, a telltale sign of addiction is lots of interpersonal problems with friends, coworkers, and family members. Anyone can develop conflicts with a few people, but if everyone in a person's life is unhappy with them or has stopped speaking to them, there is a good chance that an addiction has contributed to them alienating their loved ones.

Not showing up for dates or not keeping agreements can be a warning sign of an addiction problem. This is because addicts are often so focused on drinking or taking drugs that other commitments become secondary, and other people's needs are less important. As a result, people who are in the throes of addiction are not likely to be successful in poly relationships, because their addiction is their primary relationship and will always be prioritized.

Untreated Mental Health Conditions

Untreated mental health conditions are often a part of poly breakups. In a monogamous relationship where you live with your partner, or spend most of your time with them, these conditions are likely to become obvious quickly. But, as with substance abuse and sex addiction, it takes many poly people longer to figure out that a partner is struggling with clinical depression, an anxiety disorder, a bipolar condition, or some other serious mental health issue. In a poly relationship, you might see your partner infrequently, and you may not be paying such close attention to their behaviors if the relationship is not serious. As a result, many people are shocked when suddenly (or so it seems), a partner becomes very depressed, or has a panic attack, or seems very agitated and irrational. Frequently, this will frighten someone into ending the relationship, as they feel this is not the person they thought they were involved with. This is especially true if they don't have experience with mental health conditions, and don't know how to support a partner through such a crisis.

For example, Ray was a talented musician and the life of the party. He always had two or three boyfriends at any given moment. However, he struggled with a bipolar condition and had experienced a number of episodes of both depression and mania. He did not want to take medication because he felt it dulled his creativity and made it harder for him to write music. Instead, he used cocaine to self-medicate his depression and used alcohol to manage his anxiety and manic symptoms. He was careful not to get too seriously involved with any of his lovers, not seeing anyone too frequently in order to hide his symptoms, as well as his drug and alcohol use. When his latest boyfriend, Hans, fell in love with him and wanted a commitment, Ray tried to keep the relationship "low-key" even though he desperately wanted love and companionship. Hans eventually broke up with him after his cocaine use started to escalate and became too obvious to hide.

Another common scenario is that the primary partner is well aware of their partner's mental health condition, and has been solidly there for them, helping them through numerous bouts of depression, anxiety, mania, or psychotic episodes. They have been willing to take on this role for many years in a monogamous relationship. However, when the relationship becomes polyamorous, they feel resentful about being relegated to the role of the loyal caregiver. They may resent supporting their partner when they are at their worst, while their partner can go out and have a great time with someone else when they are well.

For instance, Kate reluctantly accepted Jane's mood swings and depression for years, even supporting the household financially when Jane had to take several months off work due to severe depression. However, she became angry when Jane started dating Gwen. She exclaimed, "I have to put up with your sullen moods and being ignored, but the new girlfriend gets the happier, more energetic version of you? Forget it!" And Jane actively hid her mental health condition from her new lover because she was afraid it would "scare her off," even skipping her antidepressant medications when she stayed overnight at Gwen's house, so when she came home to Kate she would be more depressed and unable to function.

Jane and Gwen went away on a weekend trip, and after three days off all of her medications Jane became suicidal and ended up in the hospital. By that time Kate was so exhausted from the stress, and felt so neglected that she ended the relationship. Gwen felt so bewildered and overwhelmed by the whole situation that she backed out of the relationship as well. In retrospect, Jane realized that being honest about her medical condition from the start, and sticking with her medication and self-care practices, might have prevented this outcome.

Prevention Strategies

It is important to clarify that people with mental health conditions can be healthy and appropriate candidates for poly relationships. In fact, they are often excellent relationship partners because they have years of experience with personal growth and self-care, and have been forced to learn to set healthy boundaries. In order to maximize the success of their poly relationships, it is imperative that anyone with these health conditions seek out medical care from competent professionals. Only a qualified medical doctor can provide an accurate assessment or diagnosis, and suggest appropriate treatment.

It is crucial for poly people to educate themselves about mental health conditions, to recognize symptoms in current and potential partners, to be able to offer support, and to encourage those affected to seek professional help when needed. Having more than one partner can be extremely helpful when someone is unable to take care of themselves or make rational decisions. One partner may have trouble setting firm boundaries and persuading their partner to get counseling or take medication. Having two or more partners involved can help provide ongoing support without anyone getting burned out, and partners can work together to help make healthy decisions.

Many people with mental health conditions have expressed the belief that being poly can have some strong advantages over a monogamous relationship, because in a crisis they may have more sources of support. For instance, John, Robin, and Nancy live together as a triad. Robin has suffered from depression and panic attacks since adolescence, and most of the time she is able to self-manage these conditions successfully with medication, self-hypnosis, and other self-help techniques. She has two supportive partners who give her a lot of time and attention, and she has had only one bout of debilitating depression and anxiety during the 15 years they have lived together as a family. During that six-month depression, she was terrified of being alone and cried for hours every day. John and Nancy took turns being home with her. Having two partners to share that responsibility prevented either from becoming exhausted, and allowed them both to continue working part-time to support the family financially until Robin was well enough to go back to work.

Yuri had two stretches of severe depression during the six years he was in a monogamous relationship with Michelle. He was sullen and withdrawn during three to four months of depression, and had angry outbursts when Michelle tried to coax him out of bed to go to work. He lost two jobs due to absenteeism, but he refused Michelle's pleas to take antidepressant medication, or to go to a therapist or doctor for help. He had no other close friends, and Michelle felt overwhelmed by the responsibility of taking care of him when he was depressed. He recovered, and had been doing fine for about a year when Michelle developed a crush on her close friend, Hannah. Yuri felt comfortable with Michelle's bisexuality, and consented to her initiating a sexual relationship. Over the next several months, Hannah and Michelle developed a serious love relationship, having a few overnight dates a week, and Yuri didn't feel threatened. Hannah developed a platonic friendship with Yuri and the three often spent time together most weekends playing *World of Warcraft* and other games, as well as hiking and going to movies together.

About a year into this new relationship, Yuri experienced another episode of depression. He was very irritable and

lashed out at both women over minor disagreements. He
started calling in sick to work, and was soon laid off from his
job. Hannah recognized the symptoms right away, because
her mother and two brothers had struggled with depression
all their lives. She knew Yuri had health insurance, and she
gently pressed him to go to an eight-week "Managing Your
Depression" course. Michelle was surprised when he agreed.
Hannah explained, "My brothers always refused to go to
therapy. They thought that it was a sign of weakness and
that real men don't need counseling. But they went to the
classes, since that is much more of a 'guy thing' to do. They
can solve a problem by taking a course, and learn a new skill
set." Yuri confided to Hannah that he had been feeling so
hopeless that he had considered suicide. Hannah tried to
persuade him to see his doctor, but he was not willing.

In the classes, Yuri learned cognitive behavioral techniques to help him manage his moods and change his
negative thinking, which helped him to feel more in control
and less depressed. He also developed close friendships
with two other men in the course. Both of these men were
taking antidepressants and told him how much it helped
them. Yuri talked to his doctor and started a low dose of
an antidepressant, and within a month he felt a significant
improvement in his mood and ability to function. He told
Michelle and Hannah that he finally felt, for the first time,
that he was able to pursue the things he wanted to do in
life, that his depression was no longer keeping him stuck.
Michelle was grateful that Hannah had been able to persuade Yuri to get help. Yuri said, half-jokingly but with some
seriousness, "I would have probably committed suicide by
now, but polyamory saved my life!"

At least a few poly people have said that after having
a long-term relationship with someone with a mental

health condition, they made a conscious choice to avoid getting involved with any new partner struggling with these conditions.

Brenda says, "Navigating an open relationship is difficult and complicated enough, and can be an intense emotional roller coaster even for someone with no mental health issues. It's already very challenging, and can cause lots of drama and irrational feelings in the most mentally stable person. On top of that, my husband Josh had an anxiety disorder and would have panic attacks every time I had a date with someone else. He would end up in the emergency room, or calling me in the middle of the date, freaking out and demanding that I come home. When he had anxiety attacks, he was unable to be rational, and no amount of comforting him or processing his feelings seemed to help."

Eventually, she became so frustrated with taking care of him during these frequent episodes of intense anxiety that they divorced. "After we split up, I decided I did not want to go through that again. I promised myself I would make sure any potential partner was very mentally stable and did not have any history of mental health problems. It may seem unfair to discriminate in that way in picking partners, but after 15 years of feeling so responsible for propping up another person's fragile emotional health, I just couldn't do that again."

Abuse and Poly Relationships

Abusive situations present special considerations for break-ups, whether in a monogamous relationship or an open relationship. A lot of healthy behaviors and advice that would generally be helpful in a relationship, including the process of breaking up, is *not* useful when abuse is present—and can sometimes be dangerous.

The National Coalition Against Domestic Violence reports that one in four women and one in nine men experiences some form of intimate-partner violence. This can include sexual or physical assault, stalking, or verbal and psychological abuse. While there is definitely overlap between intimate-partner violence and gendered violence against women and trans people, the full picture of abuse is far more complicated. Sadly, intimate-partner abuse occurs in every community, including the polyamorous community.

Abusive behaviors are often described as situational violence or characterological violence.

Situational violence is caused by forces external to the relationship, such as unexamined biases, PTSD-type trauma responses, past betrayals or infidelities, or other extreme extenuating circumstances. Once these external factors are addressed or removed, the abusive behavior usually stops. Situational violence can be mitigated by going to therapy, by learning de-escalation skills, and by practicing techniques to tolerate distress without reacting in abusive ways.

Luz and Mike had been married for five years when she caught him cheating with Kim, a mutual friend. Mike said he wanted to continue the relationship with Kim, and to have an open marriage, and they agreed to try it. However, Luz felt so hurt and betrayed by both her husband and her friend that she sometimes could not control her reactions and behavior. Luz tracked Mike's whereabouts with an app when he had dates with Kim. Sometimes she would show up at a restaurant where they were having dinner, calling Kim a slut and a home-wrecker, and demanding that Mike come home with her. Other times, she would call him repeatedly throughout his dates, threatening to destroy some of his prized sports memorabilia or other possessions. She called Mike's sister and told her Mike was "out screwing some whore."

They went to marriage counseling, where Luz learned to express her feelings and fears in a healthy way. Mike acknowledged that his cheating and lying had been unacceptable, and he promised never to lie to Luz again or to have any outside relationship without her consent. Eventually Luz was able to trust him again, and her feelings of betrayal and anger subsided. She was able to mend her relationship with Kim, and apologize for her threatening behaviors. Kim also apologized for her part in the deception, and offered to stop seeing Mike while Luz and Kim were in marriage counseling working to repair their trust. This relieved some of Luz's insecurities, and after a few months, she gave her consent for Mike and Kim to start dating again.

In this example, both Luz and Mike were doing the best they could with the tools they had, and both made good-faith efforts to repair their relationship. Both partners were motivated to grow and heal, which enabled them to repair the dynamic. Couples counseling, as well as individual counseling, can be a helpful catalyst for growth and change.

Characterological violence is very different from situational violence, because the perpetrator doesn't want a healthy relationship. Instead they want to exert control over their partner. The perpetrator of characterological violence in a poly relationship wields their jealousy as a weapon to keep their partner in line. Conversely, they shame or ridicule their partner if the partner experiences jealousy, anxiety, or insecurities in a poly situation. This type of emotional violence can sometimes be as damaging as physical or sexual abuse. It can be very insidious, can destroy self-esteem, and can drive someone into a suicidal depression. No amount of reasoning and negotiating can stop the abusive behavior, since the perpetrator's goal is to achieve and maintain control over their partner and the relationship.

Marilyn and Jimmie are a cohabiting poly couple. During the five years they lived together, Jimmie would often overreact and shout at Marilyn over small mistakes like missing the freeway exit or forgetting to pay a bill on time. She tried, unsuccessfully, to get him to attend an anger management group because she was not willing to accept this behavior. Then, he developed an outside relationship with Rheba, a coworker. Marilyn had some jealousy, and she went to a therapist to learn some jealousy management techniques. She got anxious and insecure, and had a little trouble sleeping when Jimmie was on dates, but she developed good coping strategies and was handling things pretty well. After Jimmie had been dating Rheba for about a year, Marilyn went on her first date with Tom, who she met on OKCupid. Jimmie was extremely jealous, and while she was on the date, he became so upset that he hacked into her account and found Tom's phone number. He called Tom and left a message on his voicemail, shouting, "If you touch my girlfriend, you'll be sorry!"

Alarmed, Tom immediately called the police, who told Jimmie that he would be arrested if he continued the threats. Tom informed Marilyn that this first date would be their last. "You told me you were in an open relationship and that Jimmie has a girlfriend. What's his problem with us dating? I don't need drama, and I don't want anything to do with your psycho boyfriend," he said.

Jimmie felt ashamed of his behavior, and agreed to get counseling at Marilyn's insistence. The therapist helped Jimmie get more control over his feelings, and taught him some techniques to self-soothe and calm down. However, he still was unable to tolerate Marilyn going on dates without hounding her with phone calls during each date, and then berating and shaming her after the date. He would interrogate her endlessly, demanding to know, "Did you suck his cock? Did he fuck you?" He told her he wanted her to be monogamous with him, even though he continued to date Rheba. This caused Marilyn to end the relationship because she was not comfortable with the double standard.

This example demonstrates a very common way that abuse and coercive control can manifest in non-monogamous relationships: enforcing behavioral double standards. While this is by no means unique to open relationships, it perhaps seems more shocking when it happens in a poly situation.

It took a lot of strength and courage for Marilyn to be able to end her relationship with Tom. In an abusive relationship, one of the most dangerous and unpredictable situations is when the target tries to leave, and the perpetrator feels they may be losing control or losing their partner. The target has good reason to fear for their own safety, and the safety of their other partners if they leave. It is highly recommended to call a domestic violence hotline or check out their websites for advice on how to plan and implement a safe departure from a violent or abusive relationship. National Domestic Violence Hotline, (thehotline.org) is a national organization offering advice and counseling by phone 24 hours a day. The Network/La Red (tnlr.org) is a 24/7 hotline based in Massachusetts for violence prevention and recovery that is expressly welcoming of all genders and sexual identities, including polyamory and BDSM. There are likely other organizations local to you that provide advice and support.

Sometimes, jealousy is weaponized in more subtle ways. A perpetrator may discourage their target from speaking to or seeing their other partners. They may sound very calm and reasonable, but have strong objections to every person their partner wants to date, or sabotage every potential relationship they try to initiate.

Janet, who identifies as bisexual, kinky, and solo poly, was in a relationship with Kane, who is in an open marriage. The relationship with Kane started out with intense sexual chemistry and involved a heavy power exchange component. Janet came to view herself as Kane's submissive. Initially, Kane presented himself as charming, open, experienced with BDSM, and politically progressive. As long as Janet went along with what Kane wanted, he easily embodied all of those qualities. However, if she ever tried to communicate a boundary or contradict him, he would immediately grow cold and withhold affection from her.

Six months into the relationship, Janet started dating Patrice, and developed a strong emotional connection to her new partner. Patrice, unlike Kane, was not conditional with her expressions of love. Whenever Kane told Janet what a horrible person she was, Patrice would counter those accusations, often citing the things Janet did well. When Patrice came into the picture, Kane became increasingly demanding. He told Janet that she was a bad submissive whenever she objected to him monopolizing time that she had set aside for dates with Patrice. However, whenever Janet asked for time to deal with a relationship issue, Kane accused her of being too possessive and jealous. Patrice began to notice that Janet's emotional state would deteriorate after every phone call or date she had with Kane, and she told Janet as much. But Janet was too in love with Kane to entertain the possibility that he was causing harm.

Janet was having panic attacks and worried that something was seriously wrong with her. Around this time, Kane went on vacation with his wife and was out of contact with Janet for a month. During this time, Janet did not have a single panic attack. She was happy and relaxed for the first time in ages. As soon as Kane called her upon his return, her panic attacks returned. This was a major wake-up call to Janet that her relationship with Kane was bad for her.

Janet was terrified to leave, but Patrice helped her, over the course of many months, develop the strength to leave. Both Patrice and Janet are in counseling to process the harm that Kane caused, and to help Patrice understand how to help Janet heal, while also practicing effective self-care. Janet and Patrice still run into Kane at various events, and when those situations arise, Patrice helps Janet minimize her exposure to Kane and manage her triggers.

When characterological abuse is present, couples therapy is usually not helpful. The perpetrator is likely to sabotage the therapeutic process, because their goal is to maintain control at all costs. Coercive control should not be confused with Dominant/Submissive or 24/7 BDSM power dynamics, which all parties enter into with fully informed consent. In the case of abuse, a partner's feelings or opportunity to consent are not taken into account, and the abusive partner demands complete obedience.

If a partner's abusive behavior has escalated slowly and steadily, the target of abuse may not realize how bad things have become without external reality checks. And because many polyamorous people are intelligent, strong, and generally emotionally healthy, acknowledging that they may be a victim of abuse is often very hard to accept. Polyamory can be a complicating factor *and* a possible source of support. Having other partners outside of the perpetrator's circles or sphere of influence can be an invaluable support, providing a reality check on the abusive partner's behavior. These support networks can help the abused partner leave the relationship.

Prevention Strategies

For all of The Big Seven causes of breakups, the two most important prevention strategies are knowing what you want in a relationship and trying to choose compatible partners.

Know What You Want and Need in a Relationship

Most people have not thought through what they really need in relationships, and as a result they don't know what they are looking for. So it is not surprising that so many people end up not getting what they want, and that their relationships don't always last.

For instance, how much sex do you reliably need, and what types of sex are necessary for you to feel sexually and emotionally satisfied? What are your core values around money and work, and how important is a potential partner's financial situation, their employment, and their way of handling money? How much togetherness and emotional intimacy do you need, and how much privacy and personal control do you need over your life? How much time do you need to be alone, and how much time do you want to spend with partners? Have you been happiest living alone, living with a partner, with more than one partner, or with a group of people? Do you want children or do you want to live with children? If so, what style of child rearing do you want? Do you feel strongly about the level of cleanliness and order in your home? Are you flexible about food and meals or do you need a very specific diet or food plan?

Knowing what makes you happy will dramatically increase the likelihood that you will be a good relationship partner, that you will articulate clearly what your needs and desires are, and that you will pick compatible partners and create healthy relationships.

Choosing the Right Partner

No one deliberately picks the wrong partners. However, we often ignore red flags that could easily alert us to potential problems, and it is best to get to know someone well enough to see these incompatibilities before committing to a serious relationship.

In the poly community, this is usually easier than for monogamists for two reasons. In the poly world, if we are considering getting involved with someone, we often know someone who has been in a relationship with that person, and can learn more about how they are in a relationship. And because they are poly, they are probably already in at least one relationship, and we may have the opportunity to see how they behave in their existing relationships, and whether they are likely to be compatible for us.

You may already be in at least one relationship, so may be less desperate then monogamous people to get involved with someone else. We poly people get some of our relationship needs met in our current relationships, so we can take our time finding appropriate partners who are compatible with us, rather than jumping into a new relationship out of loneliness or needing to get laid.

CHAPTER SIX:

Breakups Where Polyamory Plays Some Part, but Is Not the Primary Cause

The previous chapters describe the most common causes of breakups. In my counseling practice, as well as in the interviews I conducted with poly people, about half of poly breakups are caused by these usual suspects, and polyamory was not the culprit. In the other half of poly breakups, polyamory was either part of the cause or the main cause. This is important to understand, because there is an unfortunate tendency to blame the non-monogamous nature of polyamory whenever a poly relationship ends. Polyamory can be a convenient scapegoat, even when some other incompatibility or problem was actually much more influential in ending the relationship.

Let's Play High Stakes Poly Dominoes with Dr. Julie Fennell, AKA Dr. Slut!

Dr. Julie Fennell is a sociologist, writer, and polyamorist whose website, slutphd.com, has the humorous tagline "That's Doctor Slut to you!" Dr. Fennell explains that a poly breakup can affect the entire constellation of relationships connected to that relationship. She has even invented a number of extremely useful new terms to describe different poly breakup scenarios and their respective causes.

She says, "Any poly person who has a fucking clue what they're doing lives in terror of poly dominoes, by far the greatest hazard of poly life." She defines High Stakes Poly Dominoes as any dynamic in which the demise of one relationship leads (or is likely to lead) to the demise of other relationships, and says, "When playing poly dominoes, you can sometimes watch an entire string of (seemingly unconnected) relationships collapse. The epic sweep of poly dominoes across both serious and casual relationships can sometimes be breathtakingly awful." She explains, "It's the opposite of 'polytastic' arrangements, in which multiple relationships support, strengthen, and help sustain one another."

Dr. Fennell has observed that the situation most likely to cause this cavalcade of disaster is a primary triad, where each person in the triad is romantically involved with the other two. Either one duo in the triad falls apart, taking the other two relationships and the whole triad down with it, or one duo is much stronger than the other two relationships, and that couple splits off and abandons the third partner completely.

Another common scenario is one person who has two partners who really dislike each other, and one or both of them inadvertently (or deliberately) sabotages the other relationship, creating so much conflict that eventually both relationships collapse.

A third scenario is an unstable primary relationship. While even an okay primary relationship can usually survive the end of other secondary relationships, it is often much harder for secondary relationships to survive the demise of one partner's primary relationship. Dr. Fennell explains that this is "because the emotional, financial, personal, etc., upheaval of a primary relationship's dissolution often makes a person incapable of being in a healthy relationship with anyone. So much of the secondary relationship becomes about comforting the partner who has lost their primary that there is little time/energy left to focus on the relationship itself."

Another common problem is what she calls "polyunsaturation." This is the opposite of "polysaturation," which she defines as someone who has as many relationships as they can reliably sustain. Polyunsaturation happens when a person is experiencing scarcity because they don't have *enough* partners. In the context of poly dominoes, polyunsaturation usually results from both people in a relationship having recently broken up with someone. Suddenly, they are alone together without outside relationships and they start to demand more from that one relationship than it can provide, causing its demise.

Last, but definitely not least, many poly dominoes come crashing down due to someone contracting a sexually transmitted infection (STI) such as chlamydia, herpes, human papilloma virus, or plain old-fashioned gonorrhea or syphilis. Usually this happens when one person starts a new relationship with someone outside the existing poly constellation. Unfortunately, the advent of a new relationship is usually already fraught with anxiety and jealousy in adjusting to this new development, so adding an STI scare can cause the implosion of one or more relationships. Even when prompt diagnosis and treatment of those affected allows immediate enough disclosure to prevent anyone else from contracting the infection, usually the trust is broken and the damage is done. And the stigma coupled with our society's warnings about promiscuity and STIs often triggers guilt and shame about being polyamorous, causing many people to question whether they have made the right choice in being in an open relationship at all.

In my counseling practice I have seen many examples of each of the five poly-dominoes scenarios as described by Dr. Fennell, and I concur completely with her conclusions about the dangers of each one. For a much more complete and extremely useful and entertaining discussion of the topic, it is highly recommended that you read Dr. Fennell's blog.

Prevention Strategies

You can reduce your risk of playing High Stakes Poly Dominoes by avoiding some of the specific relationship configurations that are most likely to cause the dominoes to fall.

For instance, you can choose not to become part of a primary triad, or try not to date people who are in primary relationships that seem unhealthy or unlikely to survive. You can also try your best not to get involved with two people who dislike each other, and to avoid careless behaviors that are likely to cause your partners to hate or distrust each other. For instance, don't spend a lot of time complaining about one partner to the other, and avoid making comparisons among partners, as these behaviors are likely to create bad feelings.

You can increase the odds of encouraging harmonious feelings among partners by introducing potential partners to your existing partners, and giving them the opportunity to get to know each other, if they want to do so, before initiating a romantic relationship with someone new. And you can do your best to avoid STIs by getting tested before entering new sexual relationships, and having a frank discussion with potential partners about their sexual history and any STIs within their current or past relationships. While condoms, other barriers, and harm reduction practices are recommended, each relationship has its unique circumstances and risks. Only you and your partners can decide what the level of risk is in any given situation, whether barriers or additional testing are warranted, and whether to request any limits to the range of sexual activities.

Unfortunately, no amount of planning and careful partner selection can completely prevent the danger of poly dominoes sending a ripple effect of collapse through your relationships and those of your partners. However, if you are alert to the symptoms, you may be able to see disaster looming and potentially take corrective action. For instance, if you have two partners who have developed conflict or become distrustful of one another, you could suggest that they seek outside mediation to resolve these disagreements. Or you can seek individual counseling for yourself, because your behavior may have contributed to or created conflict between your partners. You may all benefit from family counseling for some or all partners, to find mutually acceptable solutions. Another option is to compartmentalize each relationship more than you have previously done, so that your partners will not have to see each other or interact as often. Sometimes just giving partners space and privacy from each other can ease tensions considerably, allowing them to "agree to disagree," and making conflicts more manageable.

If you can see that your primary relationship is developing problems, take immediate action to strengthen your relationship. Ask your partner to set aside time on a regular basis to talk about any sore spots that seem to be developing between you, and work on improving your communication together. Seek out poly support groups to get advice and to hear how other people are solving problems in their relationships. Couples counseling can be helpful if you and your partner find you keep having the same argument or have recurring issues that you are unable to resolve on your own.

Polyunsaturation is often more obvious than the other previously mentioned scenarios, as it usually occurs because you and/or your partner have recently lost another relationship. You can counteract the negative effects of polyunsaturation through increasing self-care, investing time in projects and activities that bring you satisfaction and joy, and seeking companionship from friends and family. A program of self-care to meet more of your own needs will make you less likely to become overly dependent on your remaining partner, and will strengthen that relationship. Seeking out an additional casual or secondary relationship may meet relationship needs that your current relationship is not capable of providing, which could ease the pressure you may inadvertently be placing on your current relationship.

When Polyamory Is Compounded by Other Factors

Sometimes other problems will aggravate tensions and dissatisfactions related to polyamory, and these problems can make it difficult to tease apart the real reasons someone decides to leave a relationship. Often, someone is already unhappy about their partner having other lovers, and an additional problem pushes the "cost-benefit ratio" into the negative column. One common scenario is a relationship where one person already feels they are not getting enough romantic attention because of their partner's other relationship(s), and then another problem creates even more of a scarcity.

For instance, Frances was already frustrated that her husband Joe was spending a few nights a week with his other partner, Omar, and she felt neglected and lonely. Then the software company Joe worked for was behind schedule in releasing a new product, and suddenly he was working 60 hours a week. Joe refused to stop seeing his boyfriend during the company's two months of crunch time. After another month of Joe working seven days a week, Frances finally moved out because she felt ignored and alone.

Niki was a single mom who met Kristin and her wife, Janet, through a lesbian parents group. Niki and Kristin became lovers but could only manage a couple of dates a month due to their busy schedules with jobs and kids. Then Kristin and Janet's son, Derrick, was diagnosed with Attention Deficit Hyperactivity Disorder (ADHD), and needed a lot more time and attention. Suddenly, Kristin was even less available for dates and Niki was very unhappy and pleaded for more time together. Kristin explained that she would love to have more dates, but needed to be home in the evenings to work with Derrick to complete his homework and help him with behavioral problems. She encouraged Niki to seek out a primary relationship with someone who had more time and was more available for a committed relationship. Niki was insulted, asking, "Don't you love me? Why are you trying to palm me off on someone else?" Kristin responded, "I do love you, and I don't want to lose you. But I have to prioritize my son and his special needs, and you are a mother so I thought you would understand that. You are expecting our relationship to be primary, and I am already married to someone else, and I can't meet your needs. If you had a primary partner, you would be a lot more satisfied with our relationship and its limits."

After several months with lots of fighting and no change in the frequency of their dates, Niki said, "I just can't accept feeling so unimportant to you, and always wanting more than you can give me." Ultimately, she opted to end the relationship.

Karen and Jake were a happily poly couple cohabiting for 25 years. Karen also had another serious, 10-year relationship with Miguel, and Jake had a concurrent seven-year relationship with Samantha. Then Karen's elderly mother broke her hip and became dependent on Karen to provide care several hours a day.

Karen realized she did not have the time and energy to sustain two primary relationships, and tried to negotiate with both partners for less-committed relationships. Neither Jake nor Miguel would accept less time and attention from Karen, and they both suggested hiring a caregiver for her mother, with each partner offering to pay half of the cost. She refused at first, because her mother wanted Karen to be her only caregiver, and she felt torn between her commitments to her mother and to her life partners. However, both partners insisted that this was not sustainable in the long run, and that both relationships would collapse if she did not get outside help. A compromise was reached, and Karen hired a part-time caregiver but continued to take care of her mother for a few hours every day.

Everyone was happier, including Karen, because she had been overwhelmed with her mother's care and really needed a break. Her mother actually received better care from a caring professional, who had more training and expertise, and who was able to implement important changes that improved Karen's mother's health and enhanced her quality of life.

When Pre-Existing Conditions Are Compounded by Polyamory

Sometimes one partner already feels dissatisfied and mistreated for reasons such as sexual incompatibility, or money problems, or simply growing apart. But, for the most part, they have been willing to cope with these problems for years. However, when their spouse decides to take a lover, that creates a crisis and the relationship implodes.

The most common example is a relationship where one person has started to lose interest, or feels disappointed or dissatisfied with their partner, and suggests opening up the relationship in the hope that this will improve things. Unfortunately, sometimes this is code for "I have fallen out of love with you, but I am hoping that having an additional relationship will make this relationship more tolerable," or "I'm bored with you, but I am not ready to break up with you until I have a replacement lined up." In most cases, people simply don't realize, until they start an outside relationship, that the existing relationship is fundamentally unsatisfying in some important way.

Is it a "Poly Fail" or a "Relationship Fail"?

When a poly relationship ends, it is often difficult to discern whether polyamory was the primary, or even a partial, cause. Dr. Julie Fennell says, "While polyamory itself does lead to some breakups, monogamous people demonstrate all the time that two people can do a splendid job destroying a relationship all by themselves." She believes that "relationship fails" are far more common than "poly fails." Dr. Fennell says this is often because many people who are in relationships that are on the verge of collapse for *other* reasons often make the mistake of trying polyamory as a last-ditch effort to save the relationship. She says this is "a solution that almost never works."

For instance, if a couple was always monogamous, but opens up their relationship as an attempt to mend serious problems in their relationship, and then breaks up, Dr. Fennell defines this a "relationship fail" rather than a "poly fail." This is a because the couple would have broken up anyway, whether or not they became polyamorous. While polyamory may be blamed for the demise of the relationship, it actually did not cause the relationship to fail, and it couldn't save the relationship, either. Dr. Fennell's observations and my personal experience indicate that if a previously monogamous couple ends up breaking up after embarking on a open relationship, but both partners still identify as polyamorous, it was probably a relationship fail. However, if they open their relationship, and then break up, and then both partners go back to a monogamous lifestyle after that, then it was probably a "poly fail."

As Jocelyn put it, "My partner and I met in college, and neither of us had a lot of sexual or relationship experience before our 10-year relationship. We decided to have an open relationship, we went to poly Meetup groups, and we both started dating. He fell in love with another woman, and suddenly announced that his girlfriend was leaving her husband, and that he was moving in with her. He said they had this amazing connection and that he would be unhappy if he could not fully pursue the relationship. He wanted our relationship to become secondary. I was shocked to realize that we no longer had much in common. I was heartbroken, but tried to adapt to being demoted. Six months later he decided he was monogamous after all, and dumped me to marry her."

Jocelyn's partner later admitted that he had been unhappy in the relationship for years, but could not really identify what was wrong. He really did love Jocelyn and deeply cared about her, but once he was having a passionate relationship with someone else, he realized that his feelings towards Jocelyn were more platonic and companionable than romantic, and that he had never felt very much passion or romance in their relationship.

Lila had a similar experience. She says, "I thought my marriage had lost its pizazz, but with the daily grind of kids and careers, I thought that was normal. We argued constantly, and I had a lot of resentment towards my husband because he didn't help much with the kids. And I was very disappointed in him for losing a couple of jobs due to just not working very hard. When he suggested an open marriage because I was always too tired for sex, I said fine. I didn't realize that I had lost interest in sex because I was so angry at him for ignoring my needs. He started a relationship with another woman, and gradually started spending more time with her. I was surprised to notice that I felt stronger and more confident in myself when he was not around, and realized that the constant tension and conflicts had really taken their toll on my self-esteem. I insisted that we go to marriage counseling to see if our love could be rekindled. We had some brutally honest discussions with the help of a poly-friendly therapist. We realized that we were making each other miserable, and that a divorce was long overdue. He admitted that he was terrified of being alone, and he felt he would be an asshole for 'abandoning' me and the kids, and that this had prevented him from seeing that we were incompatible."

Lila's husband says, "It was hard for me to admit that I had moved on and was in love with this new woman, and I felt horrible about leaving my wife, so I thought I could be polyamorous and have it all. However, I actually wanted a monogamous relationship and was trying to fit a square peg into a round hole, and be something I was not to try to make this work. Eventually, everything fell apart, and we are all much happier now, including our kids."

This scenario is most people's worst nightmare about venturing into an open relationship, and for good reason. However, most people who find themselves in this alarming place are not actually polyamorous by nature. They have only decided to try an open relationship in hope of improving an unsatisfying relationship, or because they are contemplating leaving the relationship but do not want to be single. Usually the polyamorous aspect of the relationship is transitional, as having outside relationships shines a spotlight on the flaws in the existing relationship and precipitates its demise. Polyamory cannot actually be blamed for these breakups, as the relationships were already very unhappy. However, without the crisis created by trying to be polyamorous, it would probably take a lot longer for either partner to be ready to actually end the relationship.

Raymond didn't realize how distant he felt from Monique until he started seeing Onyx. Monique and Raymond had been living together for several years, but Raymond felt very disappointed that Monique had dropped out of school and was only working on weekends. He had been happy to work full-time and to support them both while she was pursuing a degree in computer programming, because he felt this would help her to advance in her career, and that she would get a good job. However, once she dropped out of school, he resented being expected to pay all the bills. She had started drinking more and smoking more pot, claiming it helped her anxiety, but she seemed to be off in her own world, and Raymond felt all alone. He suggested they have other lovers, and Monique felt uncertain about whether she could handle that.

Raymond met Lulu at the Triangle Poly Dance Party at a nightclub, and they started a passionate relationship. Lulu was married, and she and her husband had an agreement that they could have two dates a week with other partners. She had her own consulting business and had a special love nest in the back room of her office for trysts. She showered Raymond with attention and loved having long talks and hot sex with him. Monique was so anxious about Raymond having a girlfriend that she drank even more when he went on dates, even though he was always home by 10 pm as he had promised. Raymond lost respect for Monique because of her excessive use of pot and alcohol, and for not supporting herself financially. Being with Onyx made him realize how much he missed the intimate connection he and Monique had previously shared, and he felt neglected and unloved. He became painfully aware that he had been settling for a very unsatisfying relationship, and he eventually asked Monique to move out.

Prevention Strategies

In some cases, the pre-existing relationship can be saved and even strengthened, even if both people in the relationship are generally more monogamous by nature. An outside relationship can serve the same purpose as what therapists used to call a "marriage maintenance affair." This means that someone starts an outside relationship to meet a specific unmet need, providing something that is missing or insufficient in the marriage, such as sex, romance, affection, intellectual connection, companionship, time, or attention. If their new partner provides that resource, they are much happier in their pre-existing relationship and satisfied enough to stay.

If you are considering an open relationship for this reason, ask yourself a few key questions to ascertain whether this strategy is likely to enhance your relationship or destroy it. First, do you love your partner, and do you really want to continue the relationship? This does not mean you have to be madly, wildly, and passionately in love with your partner. However, if there is really no love left in your relationship, or if you really don't want to be together, an outside relationship will only make that more painfully obvious and hasten its demise.

Second, do you actually like your partner and enjoy their company most of the time? Any partner will get on your nerves at times and everyone has a few obnoxious behaviors. But if you genuinely admire and respect your partner and still have good times together, adding an outside relationship to meet some of your needs is likely to improve your existing relationship, because you will be more satisfied overall. If you have lost respect for your partner and no longer enjoy spending time with them, or no longer have much in common, complicating things with polyamory will only cause you to drift farther apart.

Third, do you feel mistreated or disrespected by your partner in some important way? Any partner can hurt your feelings, say something insulting, or let you down in some way. But if you frequently feel that your partner does not listen to you and does not treat you with kindness and respect, having an outside relationship is likely to make you even more dissatisfied with them. A new partner is likely to try to impress you with lots of attention and special treatment, so that will only make your existing relationship look even worse by comparison.

And last, but definitely not least, do you believe you could be happy in a relationship that is not sexually and romantically exclusive? Some people are "monogamish," in that they are primarily monogamous, but can adapt to a more flexible relationship structure within certain limits. Monogamish couples often make an agreement that they will generally be monogamous, but with a few specific exceptions. For instance, they may agree that they can each have ongoing sexual relationships as long as they are very casual, or they decide that it's okay to have short flings while on out of town trips, or have only a long-distance relationship where visits would be infrequent. Even if you are generally happiest in a monogamous relationship, if you are comfortable with making some exceptions to the (monogamous) rule, you may be a good candidate for opening up your relationship to meet a specific need that is lacking or insufficient in your current relationship.

However, if you absolutely need a strictly monogamous relationship to feel respected, safe, and loved, you would be wise to avoid this strategy. Don't muddy the waters and create a train wreck by trying to be polyamorous if you know that goes against your core needs and values. Instead, you may benefit from couples' counseling to assess what you and your partner can do to improve your relationship, and whether you will ultimately be happier staying together or separating. A good counselor can help each of you identify and communicate your needs, decide whether you can be compatible together, and determine whether you can meet each other's relationship needs.

PART TWO:
Poly Causes for Poly Breakups

As previously discussed, about half of poly breakups are caused by factors other than the non-monogamous nature of the relationship. So what about the other half of the time, when the breakup *is* caused by being in an open relationship? In order of prevalence, the four most common causes are:

1. Falling in love with a committed monogamist
2. Picking partners who want a different model of open relationship than you do
3. Poor management of time and energy
4. Jealousy

It may come as a surprise that jealousy is the least common reason for poly breakups. In reality, other causes, such as picking the wrong partners and poor management of time and energy are fatal to a lot more poly relationships than jealousy. It is important to clarify that there is usually some jealousy present in all four of these doomed scenarios. However, in the first three, jealousy is only a symptom, and not the cause of the breakup, whereas in the fourth, jealousy is the primary reason the relationship ended.

CHAPTER SEVEN:

The Most Common Cause of Poly Breakups: Picking the Wrong Partners

Unfortunately, many polyamorous people are looking for love in all the wrong places. Either they fall in love with a monogamist, or they pick a poly person who wants a different model of polyamory than they do. These two causes of breakups will be discussed separately, because they are two very different problems. However, they have one important component in common—they both involve the same fatal error of picking incompatible partners.

Falling in Love with a Committed Monogamist

The most common reason for a polyamorous relationship to end is that one partner turns out to be a "dyed-in–the-wool" monogamist. Most polyamorous people have made this mistake at least once. Usually it starts innocently enough, especially if it is a secondary relationship, or if the relationship is not expected to be long-term. It is easy for a poly person to believe that their partner's monogamous nature can be overlooked, as the relationship is expected to be casual or brief (or both). However, a weekend fling at a conference or a friends with benefits arrangement can unexpectedly morph into a mad, passionate love affair, which may be doomed by one person wanting monogamy and the other wanting an open relationship.

Often, the monogamous person does not realize that they have a strong need for sexual and romantic exclusivity, and they only discover this irrefutable fact through months or years of trying to accept a poly relationship and being absolutely miserable. Sometimes they already know that a monogamous relationship is ideal for them, but they mistakenly believe they can learn to cope with their partner having other relationships. Or, the monogamous partner may be convinced that their partner will eventually give up their other partners and become monogamous. Usually the polyamorous person in the relationship shares in this delusional thinking. They naively believe they can convert an innately monogamous person to the joys of polyamory, but this is rarely possible.

Sometimes both people convince themselves that their love is so powerful that it can overcome any obstacle. They repeat mantras like "I'm so in love with Regina that I know we can find a solution." Or they practically get whiplash from vacillating wildly between statements like "I can put up with her living with Bill. I understand that she wants to stay married to him because of the children," and then the next day declaring, "I need to demand that she leave Bill and promise to be exclusive with me," and the next day saying, "If I just wait and let our relationship grow, she'll realize that our love is more important, and she'll eventually choose a monogamous relationship with me." They repeat this painful cycle over and over again until one of them eventually realizes that there is no happy ending in sight. Usually, the monogamous partner leaves the relationship, as they realize that no matter how much they love their partner, they will never be happy sharing their beloved with anyone else.

One client is a pretty representative example of this no-win situation. Anna met Steve at a dinner party and he was everything she ever wanted in a man: kind, handsome, articulate, loving, attentive, and successful in his career. She kept telling all her friends, "He's absolutely perfect for me in every way!" And each time her friends would respond, "Except that he's married, and you're a confirmed monogamist!"

Even though Anna knew she wanted a monogamous relationship, she fell madly in love with Steve. They spent many long nights "processing," fighting over her demands for more time and attention than he could provide. She could not understand how he could be in love with her and yet continue to be committed to his wife.

Steve's wife, Trudy, patiently supported him and his desire to make his relationship with Anna work. She volunteered to give up some of her evenings and weekends with him so he could spend more time with Anna in the hopes of satiating her need for attention and commitment. Trudy reached out to Anna by phone several times, assuring her that she wanted Anna to be happy and welcomed her into the family. However, Anna cursed at her and hung up on her whenever she called. Trudy felt she was extending an olive branch, and that she could play a helpful role in facilitating communication and being an ally to Anna. However, Anna saw Trudy's calls as intrusive and insulting. She told Steve, "Your wife is creeping me out. Tell her to back off!" Steve finally broke up with Anna when she demanded, "Divorce your wife and marry me, or else."

I have seen this tragic scenario play out many times, with the star-crossed lovers sometimes spending years trying every possible strategy to bridge the hopeless abyss between one person's need for polyamory, and the other's need for monogamy. Usually they seesaw between the monogamously oriented partner trying to tolerate their partner having other relationships, while living in constant despair and panic, and the poly partner committing to a period of strict monogamy and usually cheating. This behavior creates chaos and dysfunction in every other area of their lives, as the obsession with resolving this central relationship crisis sucks up all their time and energy. I am always struck by the intensity of their belief that their love is so important that they are willing to go through hell to try to make the relationship work, despite all evidence that it is doomed.

The same phrases have been repeated by many people in this situation. "We were meant to be together." "I've been searching all my life for her/him." "I have never felt this kind of connection with anyone before." "We are soul mates." "I've never loved anyone so much." "I can't imagine life without him/her." These phrases have become eerily familiar, as I hear them so often in counseling sessions with clients who are grappling with this poly/mono dilemma. The monogamous partner usually asks me, "Isn't there something I can do to make them happy with me so they won't want any other lovers?" Of course the answer is no because an openness to, and affinity for, multiple partners is a core aspect of being polyamorous. And the poly partner usually says, "Can't you train them to get over their monogamous programming and be okay with me being poly?" Again the answer is no because for monogamists, needing to be the one and only partner is a core part of their sexual and relational orientation.

These couples plead with me to provide them with a solution, and often become angry when I gently tell them that there is no magic bullet, and no path forward to resolve this basic incompatibility. They often say, "You're supposed to be an expert on polyamory! Why can't you tell us how to solve this?" I only wish I had a magic wand that could miraculously turn monogamists into polyamorists, or make it possible for poly people to be happy in a monogamous relationship, but unfortunately such a tool has not yet been invented.

Most of the time, one person will eventually come to their senses and end the relationship. This usually happens when they are jolted out of their denial by an external event that alerts them to the damage this unhealthy relationship is doing in their lives. For the poly person, it is often their other partner or partners who have to give them a reality check.

For instance, Kit's primary partner, Debra, seemed increasingly distant, distracted, and exhausted because she and her boyfriend were constantly in crisis over his demands for a monogamous relationship. Kit was sick of hearing about it, and annoyed that Debra would cancel date nights with him in order to reassure her boyfriend of her love for him. Debra promised Kit to honor their date nights no matter what, to be more present with him, and turn her phone off during their time together. However, she repeatedly broke this agreement, insisting that she just had to call her boyfriend right away to resolve some relationship drama. Kit felt let down that she could not keep these basic agreements with him, and felt so mistreated and ignored that he eventually ended the relationship.

In another example, Jonathan's boss told Jonathan that he was being put on probation because he had been on the phone too much and was coming in to work late way too often. Jonathan and his wife had been staying up at night fighting about his new girlfriend. He and the new girlfriend were constantly processing their relationship over the phone when he was at work, because she wanted him to leave his wife and he refused. As a result, Jonathan was too tired and distracted to actually do his job. When he realized his job was in jeopardy, and that his new lover would never be happy in a poly relationship, he decided it was best to break things off with her.

Prevention Strategies

At the risk of stating the obvious, the only prevention is to run like hell away from any potential partner who wants a monogamous relationship. This is a lot harder than it sounds. Many monogamous people think they can handle an open relationship, but discover that it triggers horrible pain, insecurity, deprivation, low self-esteem, and abandonment issues. And when a poly person is infatuated with a delightful new crush, they are not likely to heed that little voice in their head telling them that although this may seem like true love, it will create drama and chaos. Many poly people in the throes of new love will delude themselves into thinking they can be happy in a monogamous relationship. However, they usually know from painful past experience that they will eventually feel the need for a non-monogamous relationship, and are very likely to cheat.

If this is true for you, try to be honest with yourself and your partner. And when you develop an attraction to someone, you would be wise to gently but carefully question the potential partner about their feelings around sexual and romantic exclusivity, and whether this is a bottom line need for them. Don't make the mistake of believing that you can convert them to being poly, and be clear with them that you are not going to convert to monogamy. The painful truth is that a relationship in which partners have fundamentally different relationship styles is extremely unlikely to be successful.

There is a small subset of couples who identify as "poly-mono," in that one partner identifies as monogamous and the other as polyamorous. They work out boundaries and agreements that make it possible for both of them to be reasonably happy. These couples have found room for compromise, but it is only because neither partner is at the extreme end of the monogamy/polyamory spectrum.

For instance, the monogamous partner may be able to "stretch" themselves and tolerate their partner having occasional short-term sexual encounters with an ex-partner, because an ex does not seem as threatening as someone new. Or they make an agreement to have only brief flings while out of town on business trips. I have worked with a number of monogamous women who were comfortable with their husbands having outside sex only with sex workers, since the transactional nature of the relationship is likely to create very clear boundaries. One lesbian couple decided that the poly partner could attend sex parties or BDSM-oriented play parties a few times a year, and have sex or do scenes with other partners at these parties.

Some monogamous partners are okay with "dating as a couple," having a threesome together with another person, or swinging as a couple with other couples only. They often feel safer because they are present and fully participating in those experiences with their partner.

Some monogamous people are comfortable with their partner having an affectionate, "making-out" friendship with someone that does not include genital sex. Or they may be able to accept the poly partner having an internet fling with someone who lives far away, including video sex or sexting but never actually getting together in person.

These scenarios require the poly partner to significantly curtail their polyamorous activities, and to be willing to be monogamish. However, most truly monogamous people would find even these situations extremely painful and intolerable. And many polyamorous people would not be willing to accept rules that strictly limit their outside sexual and romantic relationships.

Some poly-mono couples adopt a "don't ask, don't tell" policy where the poly partner can have brief and/or casual sexual relationships with others but the monogamous partner doesn't need to know about it. This often works well for gay male couples, because as a group they seem much more skilled than others at understanding the difference between sex and love, and grasping that a partner having casual sex at the baths or at a sex club is very unlikely to have any impact on their relationship.

However, a "don't ask, don't tell" policy usually doesn't work for heterosexual and lesbian couples. Instead, it often leads to a monogamous partner suffering from anxiety and feelings of betrayal, wondering what their partner may or may not be doing with someone else. Often they start surveilling their partner by hacking into their phone or email accounts, looking for evidence that the partner has been hooking up with other people. Usually, this eventually undermines trust and destroys the relationship.

The strategies that poly-mono couples develop to allow very limited outside relationships may feel less painful and more manageable to the monogamous partner. However, in many of these "mixed marriages," the monogamous partner eventually decides that they need absolute sexual and romantic exclusivity and cannot tolerate their partner having any outside relationships of any kind. Some monogamous partners have acknowledged hoping that their poly partner would "sow their wild oats and get it out of their system," and that the poly person would eventually "settle down and be monogamous with me." Often the polyamorous partner believes that over time their monogamous partner will become more comfortable with an open relationship. It's also common for the poly person to find the agreements or limits too constraining and eventually demand more freedom. Either way, the relationship is unlikely to survive, as one partner or both people become increasingly unhappy.

If you find yourself in a relationship with someone who is demanding monogamy, but neither of you can bear the idea of ending the relationship, a few sessions of couples' counseling may be helpful. A therapist who has expertise in polyamory can help you both talk through what you each need and want in a relationship, and can help you decide if there is any way of making your relationship work. A therapist or marriage counselor is an objective third party who may be able to help clarify whether or not there is any compromise that will make you both happy.

CHAPTER EIGHT:

Different Strokes for Different Folks: When Partners Want Incompatible Models of Open Relationship

Many poly relationships end because of incompatible relationship models. There is an infinite variety of open-relationship models, as every person can customize their relationship style to suit their needs. While this is one of the strengths of polyamory, it can lead to heartache if you pick partners who want a different model than you do.

Most non-monogamous relationships fall into one of three broad categories, with many variations on each one: the primary/secondary model, the multiple primary partners model, and the multiple non-primary partners model. Each of these three models is mutually exclusive, so picking partners who want the same model is key to the success of the relationship.

The Primary/Secondary Model

By far, the most commonly practiced form of open relationship is the primary/secondary model. This is where a person is married or living with someone in a primary relationship, and any other relationships are considered secondary. This doesn't mean that they don't love or care about other partners, it just means that they will prioritize the primary couple relationship over all others. Many people find this model has the security and predictability of marriage combined with the freedom to pursue outside sexual partners.

The Multiple Primary Partners Model

There are many variations on this second model, from group marriages where all partners live together as a family, to triads, where one person has primary relationships with two separate people. There is also relationship anarchy, where any partner can develop any type of relationships with any number of partners. Most of these multiple primary partner models include three or more people in a primary relationship in which all members are equal partners. Instead of a couple having priority and control in the relationship, all relationships are considered primary. Each partner has equal power to negotiate for what they want in the relationship in terms of time, commitment, living situation, financial arrangements, sex, and other issues. However, some multiple primary partner relationships include one person who is considered the alpha, that is, they are considered "more primary" than any other partner. Some group marriages practice "polyfidelity," where they live together as a family and are sexually exclusive within the family.

The Multiple Non-Primary Partners Model

Some poly people are not looking for a committed relationship, so they prefer to remain single but participate in more than one less committed relationship. Open relationships can offer intimacy, companionship, love, and sexual satisfaction without the constraints of a primary relationship. This model works best for people who have a serious, all-consuming commitment to something other than relationships. For instance, people who seek multiple non-primary relationships are often people who are very busy with their careers, devoted to creating art or music, single parents raising children alone, on a very intense spiritual path, or full-time political activists.

Identifying Your Ideal Poly Model Can Require Some Trial and Error

Unfortunately, most poly people have to go through a few disastrous relationships with people who want an incompatible model of polyamory before they figure out which model works best for them. And to complicate matters further, some people find different models of polyamory satisfying at different developmental stages of their lives. So the model you need may change over the years, and you may find that you are no longer compatible with one or all of your partners.

For instance, many younger couples are extremely busy and focused on building careers and having children. During that period of their lives they may prefer to have one primary relationship and keep other relationships casual. When they get a little older, one person in the couple may have the time and interest in developing more serious outside relationships or even adding an additional primary relationship. Their partner may find this threatening because that doesn't match their existing primary/secondary model of polyamory.

Other people experience the opposite trajectory. When they are young, they have high libido and lots of energy for passionate love relationships with more than one partner, so they may be happiest with relationship anarchy or multiple primary partners. As they get older, they may want to settle down with one person, marry, and build a life with them, limiting outside relationships to casual sex or secondary relationships. However, the partner they want to marry may still want to continue having multiple serious relationships.

While there are many different scenarios, each with their specific array of problems, these are the two most common incompatible models:

1.   One person in the relationship wants a primary/ secondary model and the other wants to have multiple primaries

2.   One person in the relationship wants an "inclusive" model such as polyfidelity or a group marriage and the other person wants a more "compartmentalized" model such as relationship anarchy or a V triad

In the first scenario, the couple has been operating on the primary/secondary model, and agreed that any outside relationship would be secondary in terms of time and importance. One partner has a strong need to be the alpha, and they feel betrayed by their partner demoting them by bringing another primary relationship into the constellation.

A person who needs to be the alpha often cannot accept another primary into the family, and may feel hurt and angry because this is not what they signed up for. The agreed-upon boundary was that any outside relationship would be secondary. However, one partner has unexpectedly fallen in love with a secondary partner, and insists on a major change without their partner's consent.

Usually the pre-existing primary partner will respond in one of three ways: leave the relationship, sabotage the other primary relationship, or demand that their partner end the other relationship. Often, the person at the V point of this triad is in a no-win position. The newer partner feels they are always going to be less important, and may demand recognition and equal power, and the pre-existing partner might insist on maintaining their position as primary. It can be extremely challenging to find a way for both partners to feel loved and valued.

For example, Ron and David had lived together for 12 years. They had a beautiful beach house on the Florida coast that they had fixed up and turned into a bed and breakfast for LGBT tourists. David and his boyfriend, Jesse, had been lovers for six years, and spent a few nights a week together. Jesse and Ron were also friends, and the three of them often socialized and spent holidays together. Jesse was a retired teacher and he often volunteered a lot of hours to help out at the bed and breakfast during the busy season. David and Jesse were committed to each other and came to consider their relationship primary. Ron felt very threatened by this and felt he was being replaced. He insisted that David "de-escalate" the relationship and relegate it to secondary. Jesse was hurt that Ron felt so hostile towards him, and wanted David to stand up for him and for their relationship. Both partners threatened to leave David if their demands were not met.

The three of them went to counseling together for several months. The therapist was able to help Ron express his fear that David would leave him for Jesse. And Jesse was able to explain that he wanted to be seen as more than the "boy toy on the side," and be taken seriously as a bona fide partner. He felt he had worked hard for six years to earn Ron's trust, and wanted to be respected by him as David's other partner. David reassured Ron that he was fully committed to maintaining their primary relationship, and was not going to leave him for

Jesse. And Ron was able to recognize Jesse's status as a permanent member of the family. They decided together that Jesse would move into a separate apartment in their home, and would buy into the bed and breakfast as a business partner.

Sometimes a dilemma can be resolved by identifying the newer person as a primary relationship, while the pre-existing relationship is defined as "more primary," or "alpha."

It may seem linguistically confusing to say there can be more than one primary partner, since, to most people, primary means "first" or "number one." However, the reality is that many poly people are in love with one person and are in a committed primary relationship, but also *do* fall in love with a new person, and also identify the newer relationship as primary. There are some situations where the new person is considered equal to the pre-existing relationship, and sometimes that is known as having "dual co-primaries."

Such labels recognize that the newer relationship is a long-term, committed relationship, is important and valued, and that the newer partner has status and rights. However, it is also usually acknowledged that the longer history and ongoing commitment of the pre-existing relationship has more "seniority," and that the pre-existing partner has some additional priority.

Sometimes this distinction makes sense because in the pre-existing relationship, the couple is already living together, they may be legally married, have children together, own a home together, share finances, or have otherwise integrated their lives in ways that are not part of the newer relationship. Even if the newer relationship involves spending a lot of time together and even living together part-time, the pre-existing relationship may be given more time and the pre-existing partner may continue to have more control over major decisions.

Unfortunately, this mismatch of models often leads to a poly breakup. The conflict is often not just a matter of semantics, but rather about a basic differences in relationship orientation. One person in the relationship sees the couple as the basic unit of the poly family, with any other relationship a satellite revolving around that couple. The other person in the pre-existing relationship has developed a serious commitment to an outside partner, and wants that relationship to be recognized as important. They may feel that the outside partner should have additional decision-making power and play a larger role in their life. It is often impossible to find enough common ground to resolve this conflict.

Sometimes the outside partner bails out of the relationship because they are tired of feeling powerless and fighting for a place at the table. For instance, Stephanie lived alone but was already in a committed relationship with Jason when she met Sanford and fell in love with him. Because Jason was considered primary, he often set limits to how often Stephanie could see Sanford. Jason sometimes called Stephanie during her dates with Sanford and needed a lot of reassurance, sometimes even demanding that she cancel dates with Sanford when he wanted her to spend time with him instead. When Stephanie wanted to go away for a one-night trip with Sanford, Jason vetoed it. She tried to negotiate with Jason to give Sanford more time and more priority than before, but Jason felt too threatened by Stephanie having strong feelings for another man. Feeling frustrated that their relationship seemed to depend on Jason's approval and could be disrupted or changed at any time, Sanford reluctantly ended the relationship with Stephanie.

Sometimes the pre-existing partner leaves because they cannot accept a major change in the terms of the relationship and they feel displaced from their cherished role as the primary partner. Peggy and her husband, Kenneth, reached a crisis point after his once-a-week dates with his girlfriend, Nona, started to expand to two nights a week and every other weekend. He started taking weekend trips with Nona and even opened a joint bank account with her. He announced one day that he and Nona had become primary, and that he wanted to tell all their friends and family members that he was in love with Nona and that she was now a co-primary. Peggy refused to accept this, explaining, "I don't feel like part of a couple anymore. You've thrown our poly agreements out the window. You're making decisions without me and don't care about how I feel."

Kenneth said he had tried for months to involve Peggy in these decisions, but that she would not take Nona's needs into consideration. Peggy responded, "You are not giving me any control over these decisions, you're just bullying me into doing whatever you want. I am spending weekends all alone with the kids and the housework while you spend all weekend drinking and partying with her. And you are putting some of your paycheck into a bank account with her instead putting that money towards providing for our family." Kenneth would not reconsider, so Peggy filed for divorce.

Here is another very common incompatible poly model: One person wants a much more "inclusive" model such as polyfidelity, or a group marriage, or everybody's partners spending a lot of time together as a group. The other person wants a more compartmentalized model such as relationship anarchy or multiple—but completely separate—primary relationships.

In this scenario, one partner is trying to build a group marriage with a triad or a larger group who will all live together as a family, be sexually exclusive within the group, and be equally committed to everyone in the family. The other person wants to be independent of any family structure and to allow each relationship to evolve organically and rise to its own level. Sometimes this involves a conflict between the all-inclusive "one-big-happy-metamour-family" model and a model where each relationship is more private and separate.

For example, Erica and Christine lived together and had two children. Erica frequently wanted her other lover, Jorge, to spend weekends at their house hanging out with them, watching movies, going to the park with the kids, cooking meals, etc. Christine resented Jorge "intruding" on their family time and their "quality time" together on weekends. Erica often suggested that Christine invite her lover, Jane, to come over for dinners and go to social events together. Christine only wanted to spend time over at Jane's apartment, where they could have privacy and their relationship could grow and deepen without having to include Erica and the kids.

This caused a lot of conflict in Christine and Erica's relationship, as they had such different ideas of the ideal poly relationship. Jorge was convinced that Christine didn't like him and was trying to sabotage his and Erica's relationship. Christine insisted that she did not dislike him, but told Erica that, "I never promised to be best friends with your boyfriend, and I resented him always being around when I want some time with you."

Jorge had grown up in a large extended family in Guatemala, and he explained that socializing together and being a part of Erica's family felt a lot like his childhood family. He thought Christine was unfriendly and self-centered by excluding him.

Jorge extended an olive branch by suggesting a compromise. He would take the kids on an outing every Saturday afternoon and evening, to a matinee movie and out for pizza, or to a ball game or bowling. Christine and Erica could have the afternoon to do errands together, do projects together at home, and have Saturday nights for just the two of them. Then on Sunday, Jorge would spend the day with them and the kids at their home. He and Erica would continue to have their date night on Tuesday evenings at his apartment. It wasn't perfect, but Christine felt grateful to Jorge for understanding her needs, as well as helping with the kids, so she was willing to try it.

Different relationship models are generally mutually exclusive, because there is just not enough overlap in each person's vision of the "right" way to do polyamory. As a result, competing relationship models often create such conflict that the relationship will eventually collapse. Sometimes a creative approach like Jorge's can bridge the gap and satisfy enough of each person's needs that a solution can be found.

Prevention Strategies

Know what model of relationship you want and choose partners who want the same. This requires carefully thinking about what your relationship needs are, what kind of past relationships have made you happy, and what has made you miserable. Using this data from your past relationship experiences, you may be able to predict which model of open relationship is most likely to work for you. To identify your preferred model, ask yourself some tough questions. How much security do you need to feel safe in a relationship? Do you need to feel that you're "number one," or can you share that priority with other lovers? How much privacy and personal freedom do you need in order to feel comfortable? Have you been happiest living alone, living with one person, or with a group? What has pushed your buttons or been a deal-breaker in past relationships? How much time and energy do you need from partners? What level of time and commitment are you able to devote to relationships?

Some people find they can only answer these questions after trying one or more models of polyamory and discovering what their needs and limits really are. If you decide you need to experiment with different poly models, try to avoid making serious commitments that could lead to disastrous consequences if you have guessed wrong.

For instance, Javier lived in rural New Mexico, and he believed that the multiple primary partners model was right for him. He fell in love with Rhonda and Diego after initially meeting them at a munch, an intro level BDSM event, in Albuquerque, 100 miles away. After spending every weekend with them for about six months, he quit his job, sold his home, and moved into their condo. He discovered that he hated urban life and living in their small, crowded apartment. He missed having privacy and alone time. And he really missed being near his extended family. Rhonda and Diego's bickering started to escalate and become more constant, often prompting him to be the peacemaker, a role that rapidly grew tedious. He felt shut out of their emotional intimacy, because they had such a strong bond as a couple even when they were fighting. He had also taken a pay cut in his eagerness to find a job in Albuquerque, but living in the city was more expensive, creating financial stress.

All this made Javier wonder whether he had picked the wrong poly model. Would he be happier in a primary/ secondary model, where he felt more valued and was given more time and attention, or where he had more control over decisions? He was distraught that he had given up his job, house, and family for what looked increasingly like a doomed relationship.

Rhonda could see that Javier was not happy, and at her insistence, they went to family counseling as a triad. They decided to sell their condo and buy a house about halfway between Albuquerque and Javier's previous home. It was in a much more rural area, and only a 30-minute drive from most of Javier's relatives. Being able to participate fully in these decisions about moving and being a co-owner of their new home made him feel like an equal partner in the relationship. He was able to get his old job back and even got a raise, because in his absence, his employer became aware how valuable he had been to the company. Rhonda and Diego's arguments subsided, since they now had a lot more space, and everyone had more privacy, reducing tensions. Luckily, Javier had not chosen the wrong model of polyamory, but the relationship needed some fine-tuning in order to meet everyone's needs.

Many such tales do not have a happy ending. For instance, Timothy and his ex-wife, Belinda, lived in adjacent apartments in a small building in Los Angeles. Timothy had always wanted a poly relationship and while married had started a relationship with May, a poly single mother of a young son. Belinda knew she was monogamous, and as a result, she and Timothy amicably divorced. He moved into the apartment next door so they could easily share custody of their two small sons. Timothy managed the apartment building in exchange for free rent.

But Timothy and May agreed on a multiple primary partners model of polyamory, and she persuaded him to move to an intentional community that was connected with their meditation practice, which was about a four-hour drive north. Belinda felt abandoned that Timothy would not be there to share custody of the children, who felt very angry and hurt by his sudden disappearance. He drove back to visit the kids for a few days every month, trying to sustain the relationship without taking too much time away from May. He devoted his time to helping May raise her son, and worked in the intentional community managing and doing repairs on buildings, as he had done in his previous apartment building.

Both he and May had a few outside lovers, but each relationship was short-lived. However, after about a year, May fell in love with Jake, who lived in the intentional community, and Timothy discovered that he was not able to accept another primary partner into the family. May wanted Jake to move in with them and be "another daddy" to her son. She reminded Timothy that they had agreed to the multiple primary partners model. But Timothy now knew he needed to be the only primary. They split up, and Jake moved in with May and her son. Timothy was so hurt that he could no longer stand living in this small intentional community and seeing May with Jake every day. He went back to LA to be near his kids, but by this time they had grown accustomed to living with Belinda full-time and wanted little to do with him. He had spent all his savings by moving and supporting May and her son, so he was broke and unemployed. He couch-surfed with various friends for nearly a year, until he was finally able to find a part-time job, and eventually found a living situation where he could again manage a building in exchange for free rent.

He regretted that he had agreed to a multiple primary partner model of polyamory with May and had moved so far away from his children, as well as giving up free rent. In retrospect, he felt it would have made more sense to go slowly and try out different poly models to see what worked for him, and to see if he and May would be compatible, before making such big life changes.

Are You Happier with an Inclusive Model or More Compartmentalization of Your Relationships?

In trying to decide what model is best for you, think about how much "overlap" you would ideally like in your relationships. Do you prefer each relationship to be very separate and private, or do you enjoy spending a lot of time with more than one partner at the same time? What kind of relationship, if any, do you want to have with your partners' other lovers? Some people describe the "one big poly family" approach as the inclusive model. Keeping each relationship more separate is sometimes called the compartmentalized model. There is a wide spectrum of preferences between these two extremes, and most people fall somewhere along that continuum. None of these options are right or wrong, as there is no one right way to do poly relationships. For most people, it takes some practice to discover how much inclusivity works for them, and how much compartmentalization they prefer for each relationship.

For example, Howard unintentionally stumbled into a poly relationship. He was living with Marina when he fell head over heels in love with Tasha, a community organizer he met through their mutual political activism. He admits, "I had no idea what I was doing, and I lied to Marina because I assumed she would leave me if she knew I was sleeping with Tasha. Of course she found out because she saw a photo of a protest march on Facebook, and there we were with our arms around each other. She wanted to end things, and I pleaded with her to try an open relationship. I felt convinced that she would really like Tasha since they were both strong feminists and brilliant, dynamic women."

Marina agreed to try it, but she didn't like Tasha and didn't trust her because "she had been sleeping with my boyfriend for three months behind my back, and was complicit in all the lies he was telling me. I tried to like her and to hang out with them both together, but couldn't get past my anger and feeling like she made a fool of me."

Howard really wanted them all to spend time together, because they were all involved in the same community and had friends in common. Marina felt that she "should" like Tasha and be her friend. She felt especially guilty for refusing to let Tasha spend New Year's Eve with them. Howard was upset because Tasha would be all alone while he and Marina were out partying and having a great time. But Marina knew that it would be uncomfortable and unpleasant spending several hours with Howard and Tasha at a club drinking and ringing in the New Year, and she could not imagine it would be any fun for Tasha either.

Marina went to a workshop on polyamory, and during the question and answer period at the end she said, "My boyfriend is telling me I'm a bad metamour, whatever that is, because I don't want his other girlfriend horning in on our New Year's Eve plans that we made six months ago before she was even in the picture. Am I just being a selfish bitch, or do I have a right to have that holiday with him?" She was relieved when the presenter explained, "It's totally up to you whether you want to have any kind of friendship or contact with your partner's other lover. She's *his* girlfriend, not yours, and you have no responsibility towards her, except to be civil if you run into each other, and to not sabotage their relationship."

Marina felt that her feelings were being validated, and she was glad she had trusted her instinct, that she just did not want to be friends with Tasha or socialize with her. Someone at the workshop suggested that Howard could spend New Year's Eve with one partner, and New Year's Day with the other, or spend the evening with one and the night with the other, so no one would feel completely left out. Marina negotiated with Howard so she and Tasha could each have part of New Year's Eve with him, and added, "I accept your relationship with Tasha, and I respect Tasha and wish her well. But I don't want a relationship with her, and I want to keep our relationship separate."

Tasha expressed gratitude that she would not be all alone on New Year's Eve, and she admitted that she really preferred to have Howard all to herself for a shorter amount of time rather than suffer through a long and awkward night of the three of them socializing together. It turned out that she also favored the compartmentalized model of polyamory, but Howard had been pushing the more inclusive model so she thought she should try to adapt to that.

Many people make the mistake of choosing a model they think they should want, either some ideal poly lifestyle they've read about in a book, or a model being proposed by a partner, rather than what will actually work for them in the real world. Try to be honest with yourself and your partners about your needs and desires, rather than trying to fit into someone else's poly model.

CHAPTER NINE:

When Poor Management of Time and Energy is the Culprit

Many people do not have the required skill set to keep more than one partner happy. For some people, they simply have not learned to manage their time and energy well enough to be able to be a good relationship partner, and meet enough of their partners' needs to sustain each relationship. For others, it does not come naturally to be as organized and detail-oriented as most poly relationships require. Juggling two or more partners requires really paying attention to each partner's "bottom-line" needs to, at least, meet their minimum requirements consistently.

Alan calls himself a "veteran" of a 30-year poly marriage, and says, "Knowing your partners well enough to anticipate some of their needs and desires is really important." Planning ahead, and planning your time carefully is a necessity to make sure you can reliably deliver on whatever you promise each partner.

Many people lack the skills to keep one relationships afloat and keep one lover happy, much less two or more.

It takes a lot of time and energy to sustain multiple relationships, as relationships have a lot of moving parts that all need time and maintenance. And keeping your own life going smoothly, including career, family, friends, sleep, and other important activities requires good self-care. This is crucial not only to keep your sanity, but also to be able to be physically and emotionally present with each of your partners. Excellent interpersonal and communication skills are a must-have to solve the problems that will inevitably come up in any open relationship. Being able to consistently give your partners enough time and energy is vitally important to the survival of each of your relationships.

A Lot of Poly Breakups are Due to What Some Poly People Call "Kid in a Candy Store Syndrome."

Jason explains it this way: "You meet all these great people and you jump into relationships with them, convincing yourself that you have enough time and energy for three or four relationships. But then you just can't keep up that level of energy, and unfortunately, some relationships will fall through the cracks. Maybe you could handle four relationships when you were 23-years-old and didn't have kids, or a demanding career, or maybe you could manage that many relationships when two of them were casual, but then one of them becomes more serious and you can't fit everyone into your schedule anymore."

Or maybe you were giving all three of your lovers enough to satisfy them, but then a family member has a health crisis and you have an added commitment to taking care of them. Or you have a baby, and suddenly have no time for anyone. Or you get a promotion and are working more hours. Or one relationship is in crisis and needs more of your time.

Mona has been in a relationship with Jasmine for 15 years, as well as one with Martin for 12 years. She is married to Jasmine, and spends two nights a week with Martin. She says, "I found out the hard way that two relationships is the maximum that I can handle. When you're intoxicated with New Relationship Energy, you feel convinced that you have enough juice for everyone. Most poly people have found that at least one relationship will fail because they are neglecting that partner or cancelling dates on them or falling asleep in the middle of a date because they were up till 3 AM with another lover the night before. Or they carelessly schedule a date with the new partner on a day that is another partner's birthday, even worse, a wedding anniversary. I have done it and you probably have, too."

This trajectory is perfectly natural, because at the start of a new relationship, everything seems effortless in the rosy glow of newfound love. However, nine months or a year or two years later, the excitement calms down enough to notice all the problems and incompatibilities. Suddenly, the relationship becomes a lot more time-consuming and requires a lot of energy for processing and problem solving. At that point, managing multiple relationships can become quite a strain, and often one relationship (or more) will become a casualty.

Mona's wife, Jasmine, also has another partner, Cristobal, who describes himself as "Jasmine's fuck-buddy," since they see each other a one or two Saturdays a month to play pick-up basketball games at the park, and then have an overnight for sex. Cristobal underscores the importance of time management in poly relationships. "I had a boyfriend for a year who was chronically two hours late for dates or just didn't show up because he always scheduled too many things into his days, and just couldn't make it work. I had another lover who was always so busy that something as minor as getting a cold for a few days made everything fall apart, and that would create a nightmare of rescheduling and processing with angry lovers feeling neglected. Excellent time management is a necessity for poly people, it's right up there with good personal hygiene."

Most poly people have made all these mistakes and more, especially when they are new at open relationships, because they have no training or experience in trying to sustain multiple relationships.

For example, Kate felt lonely and sad sometimes, because her husband, Russell, spent two nights a week with his girlfriend, Robin. Then Russell's father died suddenly, and Russell became depressed and withdrawn. Robin called Russell frequently, asking for reassurance because he was not giving her any time or attention, and she eventually broke up with him. Kate felt unloved and rejected, and she finally threatened to file for divorce before Russell would agree to marriage counseling to try to get their relationship back on track.

Cecilia had a husband, a girlfriend, and a male lover she described as "a casual-sex date." She says, "I was the happiest woman in the world with such an abundance of love and sex in my life! But after a year of total bliss, I started feeling overwhelmed and exhausted. I realized that, except for going to work 30 hours a week, I was spending every waking hour with my husband or lovers. I started getting a lot of complaints from everyone else in my life that I was neglecting them: my grown kids, my parents, not to mention my friends, who had stopped speaking to me by this time. I had stopped writing music and stopped going to the gym because I just didn't have time. Both of those had been extremely important to me, so I knew my life was getting off track." Around the same time, her girlfriend moved about an hour away to take a very demanding job, and was much less available for dates, which gave Cecilia a little more free time. She also decided to stop seeing her male lover. As she put it, "Polyamory was never meant to replace everything else in life, and somehow relationships were becoming my whole world. My life is much more balanced now."

Some people have plenty of time and energy for their relationships, but have poor time management skills, or they refuse to plan their schedule in advance. This is particularly challenging for people who have learning disabilities or other neuro-diverse conditions like ADHD. These medical conditions can make processing information and organizing time and activities much more difficult. Many other people who do not have any type of learning disability also create chaos by being disorganized and inefficient in getting things done. As a result, they are always late, frequently cancel dates due to double-booking their schedules, or even get confused about who they have a date with that night.

Valerie broke up with Jason after they had been together about a year. She had been getting more and more fed up with receiving frantic texts a few minutes before he was due to arrive for a date, and the message was always similar: "I'm going to be a few hours late because I forgot I had to take the dog to the vet for an appointment," or "I have to cancel because I underestimated how long it would take to finish this project for work," or "Would you mind going shopping with me for a couple of hours of our date? I didn't get around to buying a gift for my son's birthday tomorrow." Valerie finally ended the relationship because Jason was going away on a road trip with his other partner and canceled his date with Valerie the night before the trip. He had not bothered packing for the trip and forgot to go food shopping for it. Valerie was irate that this trip had been planned for six months, but he had waited until the night before to do all the necessary preparations and only then canceled their date.

The Myth of Spontaneous Romance

Even more challenging than a disorganized partner is one who refuses to plan and schedule in advance and insists on being spontaneous. For some reason, men seem more likely than women to believe that they can succeed at polyamory without careful and consistent advance planning.

Forrest had three girlfriends, and he liked to make dates with each one of them on the spur of the moment. All three women were unhappy with this system, as it created chaos and uncertainty in their lives and made it difficult for them to make other plans. In order to be available for a date, they had to keep every evening and night open for him just in case he wanted a date. When they complained that this wasn't fair, he told them they needed to "go with the flow," and that making plans in advance was "too rigid" and "killed the experience," and that he couldn't predict a week in advance who he would "naturally feel like being with" on a given night. The unfortunate result was that each of them spent many nights alone, wishing they had made other plans. To make matters worse, some weeks he would spend three or four nights a week with one partner and ignore the other two, and the next week another partner might be "favored with his presence" for several nights in a row, then just as suddenly abandoned. Elaine broke up with him after three months, as she was sick of "being in suspended animation every day, wondering when I would ever see him." Rosheda had another boyfriend who was a lot more reliable, who scheduled regular dates with her every Tuesday, Friday, and Sunday nights. Rosheda told Forrest to call her only if he wanted a date on one of the remaining nights, and "don't even think about calling me on the nights I have a date with Donnie." Jillea tried to compromise by asking Forrest to call her at least two days before dates, so she could at least make plans a day or two in advance. However, Forrest couldn't even seem to plan even a few hours in advance, so Jillea ended the relationship after about six months.

Antoine ran his own business managing hip-hop musicians, and told both of his lovers that he needed flexibility because his work required that he be very available to book shows and close deals. As a result, he never made dates, but instead would call either partner at 9 or 10 PM and say, "Hi honey! Can I come over?" That worked fine for Tanisha, as she had two kids, and she wasn't really available until after getting the kids to bed, washing the dinner dishes, and doing a load of laundry. However, Eve said, "I feel like I'm just a booty call," because Antoine only came over late at night instead of socializing and going out together. She "tried to be laid-back about it," making plans with friends for dinner or a movie early in the evening, and being home by 10 PM, in case Antoine wanted to come over for a date. She was at a bar with her girlfriends one evening, and a handsome guy bought her a drink. They started dating, and he wanted a lot of her time and attention. Antoine got upset because whenever he called her for a date, she was already out with her new lover. She told Antoine, "He asks me out a week in advance. Do you expect me to say no, just on the off-chance you might call at the last minute?"

Tricia was involved with Dave, who always had other priorities that made him unwilling to plan dates with her in advance. Either he was involved in some political activism that was taking up most of his time, or he was going on trips to Hawaii to surf whenever he could get a cheap airfare. Or he would suddenly get involved with some other woman and Tricia wouldn't hear from him for weeks. She says, "Sexism is the underbelly of this myth of spontaneity that Dave tried to sell me. It's actually not spontaneous at all, because I have to be available any time and be at his beck and call. It gives the man all the power in the relationship, because I have to be available, but he doesn't. I have to have food in the house in case he wants to come over for dinner. I've got to do laundry and have fresh sheets on the bed and keep the house cleaned up because he might come over any night. And I have to make sure I always have time and energy for last-minute sex dates whenever he's in the mood to see me. And while he talks a good line about polyamory, his so-called spontaneity makes it impossible for me to have another lover, because how can I make plans with someone else when I don't know when I'll have a date with Dave? It really forces me to be monogamous, while he can do whatever he wants." Tricia did get involved with someone else, but since she was no longer available on demand, Dave stopped calling her.

Prevention Strategies

The best way to keep your relationships from succumbing to a time and energy crunch is to know your limits, and to avoid taking on more partners than you can handle. This is much easier said than done! For one thing, it is very hard to turn down a delightful love affair with a potential partner and say, "Sorry, my dance card is full."

Most people have lived through times when they were lonely and experienced a scarcity of love, affection, companionship, and sex. As a result, poly people often jump at the chance to start a new relationship, perhaps rationalizing that it's better to have too much love in their life rather than not enough. And when sexual and/or romantic chemistry with someone new is high, it is very tough to make an accurate assessment of whether you actually have room in your life for this new person. When you are just getting to know this potential lover, you don't know whether this may be a one-weekend fling, an ongoing casual affair, or if it will become something more serious, which could be very difficult to fit into an already busy life. And it's easy to conclude that if this new relationship is so wonderful, you can rearrange your schedule, or find the time somewhere because you really want it to work. That may be plausible in the short-run, but a few months down the road you may find yourself very invested in this new relationship and feeling intense pressure trying to fit it in with other responsibilities to a job, family, and other partners.

So whenever someone makes a romantic overture that you feel you just can't turn down, you would be wise to stop and look carefully at your current responsibilities and time commitments. Can you actually offer this new person enough of yourself to sustain even a casual or secondary relationship? This is a lot easier if you are out of town on a trip and not likely to see them again, or if the new lover is moving away to go to grad school in three months. However, even these very compartmentalized relationships can sometimes turn into major love relationships.

Technology has made life both easier and harder at the same time. In the past, a hot love affair at a conference or with someone who was just passing through town would likely become a sweet memory, but modern devices have enabled long-distance relationships to become more feasible and sustainable. People who live in different states, or even on different continents, can text and sext day and night, talk every day by phone, have video chats, and even have video sex dates. So even a one-night fling on a road trip or at a music festival may continue and require a lot more from you than expected. Will other people and responsibilities in your life suffer as a result? Will you be a nervous wreck, rushing around trying to live up to your other commitments, and squeezing this new relationship in somehow?

Gerald found himself in a poly dilemma. He explains, "I spent my teens and 20s being lonely and couldn't get a date to save my life. Now that I have gone to counseling and have better self-esteem and more confidence, I'm married and also have a long-term girlfriend. I still sometimes think I must be dreaming, because I can't believe my good fortune in having two wonderful women who actually love me. When someone else makes a pass at me, I am very pleasantly surprised and certainly don't want to say no to this fabulous opportunity to date a nice woman! Besides, I know how awful it is to be rejected and alone, so I certainly don't want to hurt someone by turning down their overtures. However, I have made some terrible mistakes in saying yes to new lovers, and then completely screwing it up because I just didn't have the bandwidth. In one case, I got involved with someone and they ended up hating me and never speaking to me again. Even though I was crazy about her, I was so unavailable that I could only manage a date with her once every two or three weeks, and she was always upset about that. And my wife and girlfriend were totally pissed at me for being distracted and exhausted all the time. My girlfriend would call my wife when I was out on a date with the new lover, and they would talk trash about me. Having too many people wanting you is a nice problem to have! But you're not doing yourself or anyone else a favor by getting into a relationship that you just can't sustain, and then being a big jerk to everyone."

Tava had a slightly different approach to a similar problem. She was single for years and then was thrilled to find herself in a serious relationship with Jackson. She was elated to have love in her life after a long stretch of celibacy and loneliness, but struggled to find enough time for dates with Jackson because she was in grad school as well as working part-time. About six months into the new relationship, her close friend Fern confessed to having a crush on her. Tava was torn because she was very attracted to Fern, but she barely had enough time and energy to have one relationship, never mind two. She asked Fern if she would be willing to continue their platonic friendship for one more year, until she completed her master's degree, and then become lovers if they both still had romantic feelings for each other. Fern also had a live-in girlfriend, so many of her relationship needs were already being met, and she agreed to try Tava's plan. About six months later, Tava's relationship with Jackson was more established and felt much more manageable. She was handling her school responsibilities much better as well, and was working fewer hours. As a result she felt she could offer Fern more time, and they happily began a romantic and sexual relationship. While waiting that six months wasn't easy, they were both convinced that if they had jumped into a love affair right away, their relationship would have been doomed.

Abandon the Idea of Polyamory Being Spontaneous

The reality is that open relationships generally require some advance planning, and sometimes very complicated planning. While spontaneous romance sounds great in theory, in real life it is usually incompatible with polyamory. Keeping two or more partners happy usually requires each partner knowing that they can count on regular dates, and that they can plan the other components of their lives, rather than waiting until the last minute to possibly get some time with a partner.

Some people compromise with a hybrid model that tries to have the best of both worlds, with some scheduled dates, as well as the flexibility for additional spur of the moment dates. For instance, Janine had trouble planning time with her lover, Shamine, because Janine's teenage daughter's schedule and plans were constantly changing, and her ex-wife, Brenda, often changed their childcare arrangements. So Janine made a commitment to spend every Friday night and part of every Saturday with Shamine, since Shamine always had Saturday off work, and Janine's daughter was always with Brenda or with her grandmother on Friday nights. In addition to this standing date, Janine often calls Shamine on a weekday and says, "The kids are going to a movie with their friends tonight and won't be home until 10, are you free for a date?" or "Brenda has the kids tonight and tomorrow night after all, because their cousins from New Orleans are visiting. Could we get together tonight or tomorrow night?" This works well for Shamine because she can count on seeing Janine every weekend, and often gets an extra date on a weeknight, which she says is "icing on the cake."

Angela is a midwife who is on call to deliver babies three nights a week. She has what she calls a "for sure" date every Sunday night with her lover Joey, and a standing date with her lover Josh every Monday night, since she is generally not on call those nights. Two weekends a month, she is not on call, and she plans dates in advance with each partner on those weekends. On the nights she is on call, she can call either partner that day and suggest a date, with the caveat that there is a chance she may get called in the middle of the night (or in the middle of their date) to deliver a baby.

Even people who enjoy planning ahead often bemoan the complicated scheduling required by polyamory, and feel constrained by the seemingly rigid timing of dates. Tomas jokingly told his lover Jose, "You're just here because it's Thursday, and I'm your Thursday night boy! How do I know you even felt like seeing me tonight, or did you just show up because I happen to be in your Google calendar?" Jose explained that if he didn't schedule dates with both of his lovers at least a week in advance, his life would be total chaos and he would never be able to make it work.

This is one of the seemingly paradoxical aspects of open relationships. While polyamory seems to promise wild romance and unbridled passion, it requires such a high level of organization and planning that it can seem bureaucratic and heartless.

Heather complained to Rich, "I'm just one of your harem of women, and you don't really care whether you are seeing me or one of your two other girlfriends. You just happened to schedule me for tonight, so I guess that means I'll do."

Rich struggled to convince Heather that she was special to him, and that he looked forward to seeing her all week. She was skeptical, and replied, "You're just a player! You're a smooth talker, and I'm not sure I believe you." Being on such a rigid schedule of dates with Rich every Monday and Thursday nights made Heather feel insecure and unloved. She was constantly questioning whether he really cared about her and says she felt "easily replaced" by his two other partners. When Heather wanted time with him on the weekend to go to a party or concert, or when she wanted to plan an out of town vacation with him, it was always "too complicated" for him to reschedule his other partners, and Heather gave up even trying. She says, "Eventually I started to wonder why on Earth I had a boyfriend at all, when I spent every weekend alone watching TV and ordering takeout food, all the while knowing he was out having fun partying with one of the other girlfriends." Over time, these feelings of chronic insecurity, and resentment undermined the relationship, and she eventually broke up with Rich.

Many people claim that all the planning and negotiating about schedules takes some of the romance out of a relationship. So they try to be creative and build in possibilities for being able to call and say, "Hey, I miss you and I would love to see you, if you happen to be free tonight." That can create some awkward situations, such as your lover saying, "Sorry, I am already on a date with my other partner and can't change my plans." But as Shamine says, "Sometimes the stars just align, and we both happen to be free and available, and it's really great to know that my lover is so eager to see me and spend more time with me."

The Time and Energy Management Champs

Interestingly, there are two groups who appear to be better able to avoid taking on more relationships than they can realistically handle, and who seem to manage open relationships with far fewer time management problems. These two groups are mothers of school-age children, and people over 55, who sometimes call themselves "poly geezers."

The Moms Are All Right!

Mothers of school-age children seem to manage so well because they have had years of practice juggling kids, career, spouses, and more. Florenzia told me, "We're already *used* to being insanely busy, having huge demands on our time and energy, and never getting enough sleep." And as Rosa, a mother of three says, "Poly was easy compared to what I was handling before! I was working the night shift in a nursing home, coming home in the morning and taking my kids to day care and pre-school, sleeping for four hours and then picking up the kids, getting dinner for my husband and kids, taking a nap for an hour and then going back to work all night. My husband and I spent every weekend taking care of three small kids, cleaning house, shopping, and cooking for the whole week. Once all three kids were in elementary school, life became so much easier and I was actually getting eight hours sleep! After that, having a husband and two lovers was a piece of cake compared to managing kids, a job, and a house all that time, and it was a whole lot more fun!"

Some women have explained that trying to be "super-woman"—being the perfect wife, mother, and career woman—was so impossible that they were forced to accept their limits. Laura says, "I just had to lower my expectations of myself! I realized I was never going to have a perfectly clean house or look sexy for my wife when I was running after an infant and a toddler 24 hours a day. We ordered pizza or went out for burritos a few times a week so we could have quality time together as a family. We paid the neighbor's teenager to do yardwork, and occasionally got my parents to watch the kids so we could have a grown-up date night as a couple. We never wanted to be monogamous, but once we had babies we had to take a break from polyamory because we just didn't have time, and we were too goddamned tired for sex or romance, anyway. Now that the kids are older, we've been able to resume our poly life. And when the schedule just gets too crunched, I prioritize having a date with my girlfriend or my wife over keeping the house clean, cooking, etc. Having kids has taught me that my relationships with my family and loved ones are the most important things in life. As long as I have quality time with my wife, my girlfriend, and my kids—and we can keep a roof over our heads and food on the table—nothing else really matters."

Some fathers say that their wives have been great role models in helping them learn time management skills, increasing their success in balancing work, spouse, kids, and outside relationships. Jack says, "I was always amazed by how organized Madeline was about everything. She made a list of all the tasks she needed to do that week, how long each thing would take, and what day she would do each one. She would look it over and cross out a few things, saying, that's not important or time-urgent, that one can be delegated, etc. She would cook a few casseroles on the weekend for later in the week, taught the kids to make a salad every night and wash the dishes, and assigned me to do laundry and gave me a shopping list to buy groceries. She would then schedule a weekly date with her boyfriend and negotiate with me about when I would see my girlfriend, Lorna. She often reminded me to text Lorna to make her feel special, reminded me to buy her flowers, and always remembered to put Lorna's favorite wine on the shopping list. I really appreciated her being my 'wingman' because Lorna believed that I was the most thoughtful guy in the world. I finally had to confess that I was a clueless lummox, but luckily I had a great wife who was helping me out with managing this poly thing. I thought Lorna would be mad, but she just laughed and said I was a very lucky guy, and that she appreciated Madeline being on top of everything, because she was benefiting from it."

Will calls his partner, Roxanne, "the MVP of exquisite time management." He explains, "I learned how it's done by watching her! She hired an administrative assistant, and at first I thought she was crazy to pay this woman top dollar to do what I stupidly thought was secretarial work. Her assistant, Donna, runs her business and her entire life, and does a great job of it! She plans Roxanne's schedule seven days a week down to the minute, squeezing in hair appointments, time to work out at the gym, and schedules her dates with her girlfriend, as well as setting up carpools to get the kids to school and all their after-school activities." Donna recruited a friend of hers to be Will's personal assistant. He says it is worth every penny because he has become twice as productive at work and received a major bonus from his boss. He is also much better at keeping dates with his girlfriend and is much more relaxed and able to enjoy his time with her because he is so much more organized and less stressed. He has also been able to spend more time with the kids on weekends because he is not bringing work home with him, since his assistant keeps him on track to complete tasks.

Poly Geezers Rock!

Poly people over age 55 seem to do pretty well at sustaining multiple relationships. This is probably due to two factors:

They have more years of relationship experience, and they simply have more free time for relationships because any kids are grown and they are more likely to be retired or working part-time.

Most people who are past mid-life have been through a number of relationships. They may be older and wiser than they were in their misspent youth, as they have probably developed a useful relationship skill set. They have likely learned from painful experience that relationships need care and feeding, and they have probably been through some brutal breakups. Through trial and error, they probably know much more now about what they need and want in relationships, as well as what they are actually capable of delivering. Many have learned life lessons that they can apply to creating satisfying and healthy poly relationships. And for many "poly geezers," their success in open relationships is at least partially down to having more free time due to retirement and/or to being what one poly woman called "post-kids."

A few older poly people have told me that they are much better at time management now than they were in their younger years. John says, "I lost so many boyfriends in the past because I would forget about dates or call at the last minute because I had double-booked my time with appointments. Even though I am still working full-time, I'm much more organized and better at prioritizing and follow-through than I was in the past." An older woman said, "Once the kids left home, I sold the house in the suburbs and bought a condo in the city that's very close to my job. Going from a four-bedroom house with a big yard to a studio apartment gave me back at least 20 hours a week I used to spend on housework and yardwork, and I have a 10-minute walk to work instead of a 90-minute drive in heaving traffic twice a day. My life is streamlined now, so I have a lot more time to focus on my relationships."

In fact, poly people over 55 are one of the fastest-growing demographics in the world of open relationships, usually mortifying their grown children and shocking their friends and families with their unconventional lifestyles. Some are long-term married or cohabiting couples, whether queer or straight, who have decided to open up their relationship after decades of monogamy. Others have been married and divorced a few times, and have discovered that polyamory meets their needs more fully than serial monogamy. Some have been widowed after long-term relationships, and are venturing back out into the dating world and exploring non-monogamous relationships for the first time.

In addition to these older poly "newbies," a small sub-set of older poly people have been living in ongoing open relationships for 30, 40, or even 50 years or more. Some are "aging hippies and free-love zealots," as Nancy calls herself and her two partners, Emma and Carrie. She explains, "In the 1970s, many radical lesbians believed that monogamous marriage was invented by the patriarchy to enslave women and control women's sexuality. Marriage and monogamy certainly hadn't worked out well for the straight women we knew, so lots of lesbians rejected monogamy and were trying to invent more liberated forms of love. And we thought lesbians were so highly evolved that we wouldn't be jealous, but it turned out we are just as insanely jealous as everybody else."

Nancy and Emma have been life partners for over 40 years. They were close friends with Carrie and her partner, Ginny, but Ginny died from cancer 25 years ago. The three women remained very close friends, and a few years later, Emma and Carrie fell in love. It was very difficult for Nancy at first and she struggled with anger and hurt over this new development. However, after a year of gradually working through her feelings about Emma's relationship with Carrie, she invited Carrie to "join the family." Carrie's grown daughter was distraught when she first heard about what she called "My mother's lesbian ménage a trois." She explains, "I grew up in the 1970s with two lesbian mothers, and from earliest childhood, my moms were always those freaks that everyone looked down on and snickered about. By the time I was grown up, gay people were much more accepted and I no longer felt I had to be ashamed of my family. Now, suddenly my mother has joined some crazy lesbian group marriage and I now have to explain *that* to my husband and our friends."

Bertha calls herself, Tommy, and Janet "elderly, poly weirdos, living happily ever after." Tommy and Janet are both professional musicians who met at a rock concert in 1970. They got married in what Janet describes as "the most embarrassing hippie wedding ever. It was in the woods, barefoot, I wore a homemade macramé wedding dress, and we were all on drugs." Five years later, and with two-year-old twin boys, Tommy broke their monogamous agreement by getting involved with a beautiful blues singer named Bertha. This nearly led to divorce. However, it soon had an unexpected happy ending when Janet and Bertha agreed to meet to discuss the situation. It was love at first sight! The two women bonded by sharing photos of their kids, since Bertha also had a two-year-old boy. The three of them and their kids have lived together ever since. There is one problem, however. Tommy complains that Bertha and Janet are so tight that they sometimes ignore him, and they often just make decisions without consulting him. He explains, "If they agree on something, the fix is in, and there is no point even talking about it." Otherwise, he's a very happy man.

Similarly, Jerry and Peter were already living together in 1980, when they met another cohabiting gay couple, Wayne and Tyrone. The two couples courted and lived together for 20 years as a foursome. However, Jerry was HIV positive, struggled with depression, and developed an addiction to crystal meth. All three partners asked him to move out because he would not seek treatment and stop using drugs. However, Peter continued to see Jerry and financially support him (and his drug habit). The ensuing tensions led Wayne and Tyrone to insist that Peter stop seeing Jerry, and they continued as a threesome.

Many very long-term open relationships are somewhat invisible, as most poly families have kept a low profile. For instance, Linda has two male partners, Bruce and Cliff, and they have been quietly living together for over 40 years. Bruce explains, "All our friends, extended family members, and coworkers know about our relationship, so we are obviously not keeping it secret. However, when our relationship first started, society was much less accepting of alternative types of relationships, and we did not particularly want to go on TV and talk about it like some poly people are doing now. I'm thrilled that the world has changed enough that people can feel safe being so public about their relationships now."

This statement is typical of many "poly geezers," particularly those who were in an open relationship while raising children. Many of these parents feared losing custody of their children if they were too open about their unconventional families. Danielle and her husband became lovers with another heterosexual couple in 1979. They lived together as a family for 30 years and raised two children together. Sadly, the other couple split up with them eight years ago, saying they had grown apart. Danielle says, "We saw so many lesbian mothers lose custody of their children during the 70s and 80s due to their sexual orientation. And we saw several poly families lose custody of their children during the 1980s and 90s due to vindictive ex-husbands or born-again Christian grandparents going to court and getting custody of the kids. So while we never hid the fact that all four of us were lovers, we didn't advertise it either. And when our kids were teenagers, they were totally embarrassed that we had such a goofball family, as my son called us. My daughter kept asking us how she had gotten stuck with such lame-ass parents. The kids pleaded with us to be discreet around their friends and teachers. And our son was being bullied at school because his classmates somehow thought our family was one gay male couple and one lesbian couple, when we are actually two straight married couples. I guess the kids at school just couldn't quite imagine a poly situation, but they had seen gay couples so they jumped to that conclusion."

Whether to be open or closeted is a major issue in many long-term poly families, whether or not children are involved. In some families, disagreement over this thorny issue has created such conflict that one or more partners have left the relationship. Frank and Lisa had been in an open marriage for 20 years when they met Crystal. Each of them had had several discreet outside relationships throughout their marriage. When Frank became lovers with Crystal, she was an organizer of a poly Meetup group and wrote a blog about open relationships. Their very different approaches to their relationship became a frequent source of friction during their 10-year relationship. She felt they were "too timid" for "playing it safe" by keeping their open marriage private. Frank and Lisa accused her of writing her poly blog "just to brag about how transgressive and cool you are," and that it was none of anyone else's business who they were sleeping with. Because Lisa was the director of a local women's health clinic, she was concerned that if her poly life were made public, it could be used against the clinic and their funding would be cut. Finally, Lisa started pressuring Frank to end the relationship with Crystal, but he refused. Then, Crystal accidentally outed Frank as her lover on Facebook, not realizing that she had the wrong privacy settings and that everyone could see it. Reluctantly, Frank finally ended the relationship.

CHAPTER TEN:

When Jealousy Is the Root Cause of a Breakup

It may seem surprising that jealousy is a distant fourth in the poly-related reasons that open relationships end. This is at least partly because the first three causes usually destroy a lot of poly relationships long before jealousy does. Being a polyamorist in a relationship with a monogamist, being in a relationship with someone who wants an incompatible poly model, having inadequate time and energy management skills, or taking on too many partners all cause such intense unhappiness and dissatisfaction that these relationships often collapse fairly quickly. It is possible that if those relationships lasted longer, jealousy might ultimately lead to their demise.

It is important to recognize that jealousy is present in all four of these doomed scenarios. However, in the first three, jealousy is a symptom, not the cause of the breakup, whereas in the fourth scenario, jealousy is the key reason that the relationship ends.

For instance, if you make the mistake of falling in love with a confirmed monogamist, they are probably going to be insanely jealous, because in their universe sexual and romantic exclusivity is as necessary as oxygen. A monogamist is likely to have frequent and dramatic bouts of jealousy, because the fact that their partner has another lover makes them feel fundamentally unloved, disrespected, and endangered. However, their jealousy is a symptom of the underlying incompatibility—their need for monogamy, and their partner's need for multiple sexual relationships. This mismatch of sexual and relationship orientations is the real cause of the problem, and the jealousy only shines a spotlight on that impossible divide.

To their credit, many monogamists have invested a lot of time and energy in trying to learn to manage their jealousy through classes, reading books, learning techniques, and going to counseling or support groups. This personal growth and learning of new skills can be very helpful in understanding jealousy, and reducing the pain of being with a partner who has additional sexual relationships. They may manage to reduce their jealousy enough to make an open relationship tolerable for months or even years. However, this will never solve the central dilemma of the relationship. Ultimately, the relationship will usually end, not because of jealousy, but due to the incompatible needs of a monogamist and a polyamorist.

And in the second scenario, if you pick partners who want a different model of polyamory than you, at least one partner is certain to experience intense jealousy. A partner may become very jealous because they are not getting what they believe they need and deserve to have in a relationship. That sense of entitlement is based on the structure of their preferred poly model, making them convinced that the other partner or partners are getting more than they are, or are getting something that they believe belongs to them. Anyone who wants more time, attention, commitment, or relationship status than their partner can provide will naturally become intensely jealous because they are experiencing a scarcity of the relationship resources that are central to their happiness.

This is most pronounced in the primary/secondary model, when a secondary partner who wants a primary relationship feels angry and hurt by the limits of the secondary relationship and the seeming unfairness of those arbitrary constraints. The combination of feelings of deprivation and injustice are the two key ingredients to creating jealous rage and despair in that secondary partner. However, their jealousy is only a symptom of the glaring incompatibility between the existing primary/secondary model and the secondary partner's need for a primary relationship. The primary/secondary model is mutually exclusive with the multiple primary partners' model desired by this secondary partner. The secondary partner will aggressively advocate for a primary relationship, demanding equality with their lover's primary partner. Their lover (and the primary partner) will struggle to hold their boundaries and force the relationship to remain secondary. This constant tension and power struggle will eventually exhaust everyone in this relationship constellation, and usually no amount of compromise will satisfy everyone. This impossible gap between what the secondary partner wants and what their partner can give them will inevitably cause the demise of this relationship.

And if you have poor time and energy management skills, or if you get involved in more relationships than you can realistically sustain, your partners may also become jealous because they are not getting enough attention. They may be starving for love and affection and feel neglected, which is a surefire recipe for creating jealousy. Each partner may mistakenly believe that the other partner or partners are getting more time, attention, and status than they are. They may envy the other partners and covet what they believe they have.

For instance, Clarissa envied her partner Jason's wife, Selena, because she had all the "privileges" Clarissa craved: living with him, sharing finances, and being close to his family. She coveted Selena's status of being legally married to Jason and being recognized publicly as his wife. However, Selena experienced frequent and intense bouts of jealousy because Jason spent two nights a week with Clarissa and at least two nights a week with his other casual lovers. He was so distracted and tired from all these extra-marital adventures that when he was home he just wanted to play video games or fall asleep on the couch watching TV. Selena envied Clarissa having romantic dates with Jason, going out to dinner, going out dancing, and she suspected that they were constantly having wild sex while he was always too tired for sex when he was home with her. She felt totally abandoned and alone, and longed for the kind of exciting love affair that she imagined Clarissa had with Jason. Both Clarissa and Selena believed that the other was getting a much better deal, and that created very painful jealousy for both of them.

However, the real cause of the problem was that Jason did not really have enough time and energy to make these relationships work, and he did not take the necessary steps to give each of his partners the attention they needed. So when Selena finally filed for divorce, it was because she was feeling so starved for Jason's time and love, not because of jealousy. She had become convinced that he was unwilling or unable to prioritize her needs and spend quality time with her. Again, jealousy was a symptom of the dysfunction in the relationship, and not the actual cause of the divorce.

Three Ways Jealousy Can Destroy Poly Relationships

In the first three types of poly breakups, jealousy is a symptom of the dysfunction, but not the cause of the relationship's demise. In this fourth set of scenarios, jealousy is the root cause of the breakup. This assumes that each person is a reasonably healthy relationship partner, and behaving pretty well, but even so, at least one partner is still experiencing intense jealousy, which causes the relationship to collapse.

In other words, you can be doing everything "right" and still have a jealousy problem. You have picked partners who are non-monogamous by orientation. You have chosen partners who want the same model of polyamory that you do. You have excellent time and energy management skills, and you are pretty much consistently delivering the amount of time, attention, and commitment you have promised each partner. However, despite your best efforts to be a poly poster child and relationship role model, jealousy remains so unbearable that one of your relationships collapses.

Jealousy as the Three-Headed Dog from Hell

When jealousy destroys a polyamorous relationship, one or more of three factors are to blame. First, people are generally not very good at cooperatively sharing *any* resource, never mind sharing their lover or spouse's affections. Second, most cultures train people to believe they are entitled to their partner's sexual and romantic fidelity, and they are expected to feel outraged, betrayed, and mistreated if their partner has other partners. As a result, most people have internalized that programming and it can be very tough to override. Third, most people have at least some amount of insecurity, self-esteem issues, fear of abandonment, and some lingering doubts about their desirability as a spouse and sexual partner. After all, who among us is such a perfect mental health role model that we are totally confident about ourselves and wholly convinced that we are a fantastic life partner and lover? Any of these three factors is likely to generate intense jealousy. Frequently, all three conspire to create such a toxic mix of anxiety, anger, and despair that the relationship will fall apart. Celina called this "the three-headed dog from hell that ruined my life."

She and her partner, Aidan, were part of a radical political collective that rented a house together. She and Aidan were very much in love, and they had opened their relationship to other lovers after two years of what she called unintentional monogamy. "We were just so into each other that we weren't interested in anyone else for the first few years," she says. They both wanted the multiple primary partners model. Neither of them enjoyed casual sex, and since they were anarchists, they opposed hierarchical concepts and abhorred the idea of anyone being called secondary. Aidan fell in love with Marta, another woman who was part of their collective household, and Celina became very involved in a serious relationship with Paz, a political comrade who lived nearby. For several months they were both so enamored with their respective new lovers that they did not experience very much jealousy.

However, Celina says, "There was trouble in poly paradise. Marta was very attractive and was well-respected in the community for starting worker-owned cooperative businesses. One day she was interviewed on TV about a new co-op, the interview went viral on the internet, and suddenly she was famous and important! I started to compare myself to her and felt really inferior and insecure. I became so needy for reassurance that Aidan was sick of me asking him if he loved me, and my demanding that he promise not to leave me. He just kept telling me how ridiculous my fears were, and of course that made me feel even worse.

"I made the mistake of telling my mother about the situation on the phone, and she immediately started in with anti-poly rhetoric about how I was in an abusive relationship and I should get out immediately. All through my childhood, my father had cheated on her and that eventually caused their divorce. My mom was insanely jealous and would catch him in affairs and go totally ballistic. She had indoctrinated me all my life that a man should be faithful and that no woman should put up with a man sleeping with another woman. I knew that what she was saying was her truth and not mine, but in my very vulnerable state, that old programming kicked in, and my jealousy went off the charts. I tried to get a grip, but then my mom told my sister and she called me, saying, 'It's every woman for herself! That bitch is trying to steal your man! He belongs to you, so go claim him!' I bought into those fears that being cooperative and sharing your lover is being a damn fool, and I became possessive and controlling. This alienated Aidan even more. Paz tried to be loving and supportive, but he got fed up because I was such a mess, freaking out and ranting about Aiden all the time. Paz eventually got tired of this drama and broke up with me, so I demanded that Aidan break up with Marta. That was the last straw; he broke up with me instead."

In a state of shock over losing both of her relationships, Celina started seeing a therapist who shared her radical political views and who had expertise in open relationships. Over time, she was able to see how she and Aidan had been trying to do something that was very challenging, and for which they had no training or experience to guide them. She says, "Believing in cooperation and sharing resources is so foreign to the competitive and dog-eat-dog model we have been taught in the Western world. And sharing your beloved with another partner is even more far-fetched and there is no support for it in society. And I did not realize that my family had really indoctrinated me with that monogamous relationship model so completely. And with Marta suddenly being a social media star, all my own feelings of inadequacy really kicked in and made me feel like a loser, and I just started acting so crazy that no wonder both my partners dumped me!"

While Celina's experience was especially painful and dramatic, it is, unfortunately, not unusual for all three of these factors to feed on each other and destroy a relationship. If only one component is affecting the relationship, it may do a lot of damage, but with time and effort, often the relationship can survive. If two of them or all three are activated, it is often fatal to the relationship. Each of these three will be discussed separately, but most of the time at least two or more phenomena coexist, and combine to drag down everyone in their path.

Homo Sapiens Totally Suck at Sharing

Homo sapiens as a species tend to be territorial and extremely possessive of resources of all kinds, including relationships. It's probably one of the larger understatements in history to say that humans are not good at sharing. We clearly have a terrible track record when it comes to sharing resources, whether they are land, housing, food, water, fuel, minerals, labor, money, weapons, political or decision-making power, or any other resource. Real or imagined competition for resources is a key reason humans perpetually engage in warfare. Humans always seem to believe that we don't have enough. We may experience a real scarcity of resources, or believe someone has more than we do, something better than we do, or something that we feel we deserve and must have. This worldview fosters a culture of jealousy and encourages us to fiercely guard any and all resources that we already have, and to try to procure those that we don't yet possess.

Millions of people around the world *do* suffer from scarcity, lacking access to adequate food, potable water, health care, education, and housing. Deprivation of the necessities of survival naturally creates intense competition for resources. However, in the so-called "developed" nations of North America and Europe, many of us have ample resources, particularly compared to people in the global south. However, we are so frightened of not having enough, or of losing something we have, that we tend to hoard what we have and not share our surplus.

Humans seem especially unskilled at sharing a spouse or lover with another partner. A very primal experience of envy, jealousy, and/or coveting is provoked by that need to own and possess everything, including a partner. Some people have argued that political systems such as capitalism are partly to blame, as they emphasize and reward individualism, selfishness, and greed, instead of cooperation, community building, and working for the greater good. Our political and economic system is built on creating a fear of scarcity, and encourages each person to try to accumulate wealth and power for themselves, teaching us that this is the only path to physical safety, economic security, and abundant resources.

The entire advertising industry, for example, exists solely to convince us that we absolutely must buy lots of products in order to be happy, regardless of the actual usefulness or necessity of those products.

Some evolutionary biologists, such as David Buss, have done extensive research on jealousy. They have concluded that jealousy is hardwired in humans, because in our ancient past, it had a survival benefit. Dr. Buss is convinced that over millions of years of evolution, people who were jealous engaged in "mate guarding," a range of possessive and surveilling behaviors that prevented their partners from having sex and procreating with anyone else. These jealous people were more likely to successfully reproduce and pass on their genes, including a predisposition towards intense jealousy. Because people who were not jealous were not as hypervigilant, the more jealous people were able to "poach" their mates and ultimately have more offspring. This makes it more likely that jealous people will pass on this tendency to their children, and this has caused humans to become *more* jealous over millennia, rather than less.

Dr. Buss and other scientists have theorized that this possible biological component could help explain why jealousy can be so intense and so seemingly irrational. They cite many instances where jealousy has led to battery and murder of a suspected or actual unfaithful partner, speculating that these extreme and violent reactions cannot be explained by psychological factors alone. More research may add to our understanding of the horrific consequences of jealousy. And it may be impossible to separate the complex interplay of nature and nurture in the development of jealousy, as most cultures explicitly encourage and condone jealous attitudes and behaviors.

Most Cultures Encourage and Normalize Jealousy

The second reason jealousy destroys so many relationships is that we are practically indoctrinated from birth, by a coercively monogamous culture, to feel entitled to our partner's sexual and romantic fidelity. We are encouraged to experience jealousy about our partner's real or perceived attraction towards anyone else, and our socialization trains us to respond with anxiety, anger, and even violence.

The expectation of jealousy seems to be so deeply ingrained that many people are incredulous if anyone exhibits an absence of jealousy. Polyamorous people have reported being told that if they don't feel jealous, they must not love their partner, or they obviously don't care about the relationship. Janet explains, "I spent years struggling with my jealousy and getting therapy and reading everything I could find on how to manage and overcome jealousy in an open relationship. I finally got a handle on it after a lot of hard work and lots of horrible pain! I began to feel confident that when my partner was out on dates with his other lover, I could enjoy having the time to myself or going out with friends or family. But everyone kept saying things like, 'Aren't you upset? You seem so indifferent that Jim is out with his girlfriend,' and, 'What's wrong with you, why aren't you angry about this?' or, 'Wow, you should be pissed off!' and made me feel like I was a bad wife for being okay with it." Ken had a similar experience. "I should never have told my male friends that my life partner, Holly, had another boyfriend," he says. "Every time I saw them, they would give me a hard time about how I was a doormat for 'letting her get away with that' and that she was really mistreating me and I shouldn't tolerate it. One of them kept saying that since I didn't mind her being with another man, I obviously didn't care about her. Another friend, who is a psychologist, kept saying I was just in denial about my feelings! The fact is, I did have a lot of jealousy in the beginning, and would get very anxious when she was on a date. But now I feel very secure about our relationship, and she has been very proactive about helping me feel safe and loved. I know she is not going to leave me, and her other relationship has not changed anything about our relationship, so I don't need to be jealous anymore. She has been seeing him for several years, and it really doesn't feel any different now when she goes out with him than if she is out with her girlfriends."

Ralph Hupka, a cross-cultural psychologist, has undertaken extensive studies of jealousy in a wide variety of cultures around the world. He found that people in all cultures experience jealousy, whether Indigenous cultures in remote villages or others in small towns or big cities, whether rich or poor, regardless of race or religion, and in Western countries as well as in developing nations. He concludes that jealousy appears to be a universal emotion worldwide. However, his research identified fascinating differences in the experience and manifestations of jealousy depending on cultural expectations. Some cultures encourage jealousy and condone jealous behavior much more than others, and some cultures expect jealousy in some situations and not others. And some cultures acknowledge, validate, and normalize feelings of jealousy, but seriously frown on "acting out" jealous behaviors.

Anthropologist Leanna Wolfe has done extensive research on jealousy in polygamous cultures in West Africa. In rural villages in some African nations, polygamy is common, and men often have two or more wives. Dr. Wolfe found that while each wife is expected to experience some jealousy towards her husband's other wives, the culture

encourages her to develop a friendly and cooperative relationship with her co-wives. Interestingly, jealous feelings
and behavior are less likely to be provoked by the husband's
sexual and romantic relationships with the other wives.
Instead, jealousy is almost always a response to a husband
failing to provide adequate resources to each wife and her
children. For instance, if he gives one wife more livestock,
more land, or a better house than another wife, the wife
with fewer resources is expected to be jealous and demand
equal support. Or if another wife's children are favored over
her children, she would become jealous and demand that
her children be given equal status and resources. Dr. Wolfe
notes another factor that seems to be crucial in reducing
jealousy: The co-wives work together farming, taking care
of children, and preparing meals. They are an important
support system for each other. This is especially true if one
wife is ill or injured, or is pregnant and cannot do as much
of the heavy work, in which case the other wives carry
her workload.

Hupka found that in certain cultures, jealous behaviors
are expected and condoned only to "save face" when someone is publicly humiliated by a partner's extra-marital affairs.
For instance, he found that in some Asian cultures, many
middle class and affluent men have a female lover outside of
their marriage. He says that most wives will assume that the
husband has a girlfriend, whom he is likely to be supporting
financially. Most wives accept this arrangement, as long as
the husband keeps the other relationship private from their
community, and does not spend too much money supporting her. If he is careless and the truth comes out, this creates
a public relations problem for the wife, as she feels publicly
disgraced and her status is lowered in the community and
with her family. In this situation, she is expected to be angry

and jealous, and only under these circumstances is it socially acceptable for her to divorce him.

In Japan, according to some research, many gay and bisexual men still marry women, but have concurrent long-term relationships with men. According to scholars Sachiko Ishino and Naeko Wakabayashi, these arrangements are accepted by the wives with little jealousy, as long as the same-sex relationship is kept private, the marriage produces children, and the husband financially supports his family. The wife is only expected to become jealous and act out that jealousy if the same-sex relationship becomes public and causes a scandal, which may mar her reputation and lower the whole family's social status.

The research done by many scholars and anthropologists indicates that these nuanced attitudes and behaviors around jealousy are largely learned, due to the cues and cultural norms in each society. However, there are big differences in which situations and circumstances provoke the most jealousy, and whether (and in what ways) jealousy is expressed.

Insecurities, Self-Doubts, and the Curse of Comparing Yourself to Someone Else

The third way that jealousy destroys relationships is through our own internal insecurities and doubts about our value as a person, and our desirability as a relationship partner. Whether we like to admit it or not, most of us have self-esteem issues, fear of abandonment, and some lingering doubts about our worthiness as a spouse and sexual partner. Very few people have stellar emotional health and feel totally confident and wholly convinced of being an ideal life partner and lover. And most people have been cruelly dumped by at least one previous partner, leaving some nasty wounds in our self-esteem and feeding our fears that it could happen again in a current relationship.

In an open relationship where your partner has other partners, this can lead to a primal experience of jealousy when we compare ourselves to another partner and believe that we come up lacking. For example, Das says, "Well of course I was just sure that Ali would leave me for this new guy, Gerald! After all, he has a bigger IQ, a bigger bank account, a bigger motorcycle, and a bigger dick than me!" Ali tried to remind Das that he was committed to their relationship and was not impressed with any of the things Das thought were so persuasive. "When have I ever cared about money or someone being a brilliant genius? And I don't even like motorcycles, I'm not riding on his goddamn motorcycle! And you have a very active imagination, dude. What makes you think he has a big dick? You've never even seen it!"

Das felt Ali might be impressed with Gerald being a scientist and having a PhD from Harvard, or because he could afford a fancy custom-made motorcycle, but Ali reminded him about all the times they had both made fun of his pretentious coworkers who bragged about their Ivy League degrees, and their expensive vacations skiing in the Alps. "Oh yeah, I forgot!" said Das, "You always text me a 'pompous-ass alert' when one of them is starting in pontificating about something they just bought or something they have done that they think is so important!"

Ginny had similar fears about her husband's girlfriend, Lynne. Ginny was shy and quiet, and had a steady job as an accountant. She feared that she would seem dull and dreary in comparison to Lynne, who was a voice actor and ran her own business managing other actors who did voice work for TV and radio commercials. Ginny had always felt inferior to other women, whom she felt were more vivacious, charming, and socially at ease. Ginny was always nervous around people and felt she didn't have much to add to conversations. "Why would he stay with me when he could have this exciting woman who was so self-confident and the life of the party?" She angrily confronted her husband, saying, "I bet you would rather spend all your time with her since she's so fun and fascinating." Her husband was shocked, and reminded her that he liked stability and calm in his home life, and that he felt very safe and happy with her. He explained that while he loved dating Lynne, "I enjoy her in small doses, and being around that frenetic energy and constant social whirl just wears me out and becomes very irritating pretty quickly. I love spending most of my time with you, and seeing her once in a while." It was very reassuring for Ginny to hear that her husband appreciated her good qualities and was not eager to throw her overboard for Lynne.

Brianna says, "It took me years to realize that my partner was not going to leave me for someone else. I was so busy imagining worst-case scenarios that it probably took me 10 years to notice that Roy had dated five other women during that decade and had never shown any signs of leaving me for any of them. It finally dawned on me that yes, from a completely objective standpoint, each of those women was prettier and sexier than me, and each of them was clearly smarter and more talented than me, and for all I know they all gave better blow jobs than I do. But *duh*!! He did *not* leave me and he's not going to. The fact is that even though these women were 'better' than me in so many ways, he loved me for who I was and he wanted to be with me." She had to chuckle when her therapist pointed out that most people do not make long-term decisions about relationships based on a simple checklist of how smart, rich, or good-looking a partner is. Choosing to stay in or leave a relationship is based on a very complex combination of history, investment, attachment, chemistry, companionship, loyalty, and personality. As the therapist put it, "People don't choose a spouse like buying a house, where you might buy a small, inexpensive, starter house and then later, trade up to a bigger, more expensive house. Love and relationships don't really work that way."

Brianna says, "I just assumed that any reasonable person would throw me under the bus if someone better came along, but I realized that it's not that simple, because relationships are not strictly transactional." She had been living in fear because, "I knew that no matter how fabulous you are, there will always be someone more attractive than you are, in some way, shape, or form. So I just had to get over myself!"

Sylvia had a similar reaction. She had panic attacks and had to take Ativan when her wife, Rita, went out on dates with other women. Because Rita always seemed to pick much younger, very attractive women for secondary partners, Sylvia was convinced that Rita was auditioning her replacement. She knew she was in trouble when she had so much anxiety that she ended up in the emergency room with heart palpitations. She took a meditation class, and started meditating every day. She went to a therapy group for people struggling with anxiety, and learned some cognitive behavioral techniques to manage her anxiety. She started going to a queer women's poly group to talk with other women about how they handled their jealousy. To explain to the other women in the group just why she got so upset, she showed them photos of the other women her wife had been dating. Sylvia was quite surprised at the reactions of the other women in the group. Instead of being sympathetic and comforting her, one woman said, "Wow, she's so hot! Your wife must be pretty amazing to be dating her!" Another responded, "Yeah, Rita must really be a catch, you must be so proud to be with her!" A third one said, "And you obviously are really great if she married you." Sylvia suddenly realized that her wife's ability to attract these gorgeous young women was something to admire and respect. All along she had felt that this meant she was inferior and inadequate as a partner. Now she was able to grasp that it actually reflected quite favorably on her, that such an incredible woman had chosen her as her life partner. "Suddenly I started to feel special and lucky to be with Rita, rather than the pathetic loser I had been convinced I was," she says.

Prevention Strategies

Many polyamorous people believe that jealousy is a normal, natural response that serves a valid purpose. It is provoked when we feel threatened with loss of something precious to us, and alerts us to pay attention to our relationships, to make sure they are safe and sound. Like a smoke alarm that may go off when you just burn the toast, jealousy may sometimes be an overreaction. When the alarm goes off, it makes you pay attention and check that the house is not on fire, and if it is just burned toast, you can relax. However, if the house is on fire, or your relationship is in danger, you can take whatever steps are needed to put out the fire, salvage what you can, and possibly rebuild, or to strengthen your relationship and see if the damage to it can be repaired.

In an open relationship, it is important to recognize that any new outside relationship is a potential threat to the survival of your relationship. A new relationship is not a threat per se, but any new relationship has the *potential* to disrupt, destabilize, or destroy your relationship. Anyone who has been in an open relationship, or been around polyamorous people for any length of time, has seen situations where a new relationship did, in fact, destroy an existing relationship. So it is foolhardy to make believe that this could never happen to you. Instead, make jealousy your protective ally, and pay attention to jealous feelings, as they can encourage you to closely look at what is going on in your relationship, and continue to assess whether there is cause for concern, or whether you can turn down the jealousy alarm.

While everyone has some insecurities and fears, there are many people who have more intense anxiety, low self-esteem, and abandonment issues, which are guaranteed to generate jealousy. In particular, people who have anxiety and a poor self-image are not ideal candidates for open relationships, because it will require a lot of hard work to improve their self-esteem and reduce their fears. Even people with *no* anxiety and great self-esteem experience a fair amount of fear and insecurity in a polyamorous relationship, because it is so challenging to sexually or romantically share our partner. And maybe this is not such a bad thing. Polyamory pioneer Deborah Anapol says in *Polyamory in the 21st Century*, "Do you really want anyone who is so securely arrogant as to be immune to jealousy?" She suggests that for someone to experience *no* jealousy at all, they must be convinced that they are so perfect that no one else could possibly threaten their primacy. Maybe it makes sense to be humble enough to realize that we can't really be certain that no outside partner could ever tempt a partner to displace us.

However, most people have the opposite problem. The vast majority of people already have some lingering doubts about their worthiness and desirability. And for those who already experience high anxiety in life in general, it can be much harder to feel safe and loved in a poly relationship. So they will have to work much harder to overcome their fears of abandonment and their negative beliefs about themselves.

In interviewing poly people about their experiences, I found that many people stressed the importance of investing in learning jealousy management skills. Many also reiterated how helpful it had been for them to examine and deconstruct some of their core beliefs about relationships that had created insecurities and jealousy. For others, the most important task was to have counseling to improve their self-esteem and learn skills to better manage their anxiety when a poly situation triggered intense emotions. While it may seem oversimplified, this is the take home message: The stronger and more comfortable you are with yourself, and the more confident you feel in your own value as a person and a partner, the less jealousy you will experience, and it will be more manageable when it does inevitably occur.

PART THREE:
Surviving a Poly Breakup

Why Are Poly Breakups So Excruciatingly Painful?

Many people have been shocked by the intensity and longevity of the pain caused by the demise of their polyamorous relationship. Many confess that they expected it to be easier, rather than harder, than a monogamous breakup.

Karen says, "I could not believe that I fell into a practically comatose state and wanted to die after Jerome left me! I was outraged because his wife was so paranoid she thought I was trying to replace her. I was in love with him, but I kept reassuring her that I already have a husband, I'm not trying to take yours. Jerome couldn't handle the poly drama and broke things off with me, and I thought it would not be this bad. My husband, Alan, was very supportive, as he had been through a few rough poly breakups with girlfriends. We had been through a lot together because my husband is transgender and I was with him during that transition, every step of the way, from Alice to Alan. But I was so depressed, and pining for Jerome, and felt so betrayed by him for abandoning me. I understood that he felt he had to choose his marriage over me. But I was also furious at him, because it was totally unnecessary for him to end our relationship—it was never a threat to his marriage. The unfairness and stupidity of that made me so mad at him, and at her, too!"

Karen and Alan attended a support group for couples in open relationships, and many of these couples described similar feelings and experiences. Karen was relieved to hear one man say, "I thought a poly breakup would be a piece of cake, because I still have a wife who loves me and will be there for me. When I went through a divorce in a monogamous relationship, suddenly I was single, facing an empty dinner table every night, and sleeping alone for the first time in 10 years. With this poly breakup, I was so, so sad for months, and could barely function at work. I could barely talk to my wife, Joni, without remembering Sarah and knowing I would never see her again. It just didn't make sense, but being with Joni just seemed to make the longing for Sarah worse, and I felt so guilty about that. It took six months for me to really be able to be fully present with Joni, and be a normal husband again, instead of an embarrassing sad sack who was an emotional wreck who starts crying during sex." Karen says, "This made me realize that I was not crazy to be in such a pit of despair over losing Jerome, and I felt less guilty about not being 100% present for Alan right away."

One of the reasons for this reaction is that when you experience the ending of a monogamous relationship, you become single and have the solitude and space to grieve the loss of your beloved. Addie puts it this way, "You can cry and retreat, pull the curtains and hide out in your apartment, and lick your wounds. You have the privacy to spend your time obsessing about your ex, navel-gazing, and speculating about why this relationship didn't work out. And if you're still talking to your ex, you can spend hours processing endlessly with them about the relationship and its demise. You can be furious with your ex-partner and talk to all your friends about what a jerk they are and how mistreated your feel."

If you are poly, when one relationship ends, you proba-bly don't have the option of just falling apart. Usually, there is at least one surviving relationship that needs care and feeding. Through my counseling practice, as well as in interviews with polyamorous people, I found that there are four key survival skills needed to get through a poly breakup: self-care, grieving your losses and understanding any lessons that can be learned from this situation, sustaining your other relationships, and handling the public relations. The next four chapters outline each of these skills and attempt to provide a guide to eventual recovery.

CHAPTER ELEVEN:

Self-Care Is the First Step to Surviving a Breakup

There is no simple road map for getting from heartbreak to happy. However, there is a lot you can do to move through this painful loss and gradually recover your equilibrium and joy. The following chapters focus on a four-pronged plan to take care of yourself, learn what you can from the past relationship, successfully maintain your other relationships, and handle other people's reactions.

Many books have been written about how to get over the pain of a lost love, and most of those books have at least some useful advice that can benefit anyone weathering the end of a relationship, whether monogamous or poly. This book does not attempt to present a complete primer on surviving a breakup. However, the end of a poly relationship creates some unique challenges that require some creative solutions tailored to the polyamorous nature of the relationship.

Ways of Taking Care of Yourself

"Self-care" covers a lot of territory and will look different for each person based on individual needs and desires, but it includes all the activities and behaviors you engage in to heal yourself after a painful ending to a valued relationship. This can mean reaching out to friends and family for support, joining a support group, or going to counseling. It could involve making art or music, playing sports, knitting or crafting, or any other hobbies or leisure activities that you enjoy. It could be spending time in nature or taking a vacation. For some people, taking a class or learning a new skill is very healing and restores self-esteem. Others may find great comfort through nurturing themselves with a massage, a nice dinner out, a new haircut, a weekend ski trip, or new carpentry tool. Don't judge yourself during this very painful period of recovery. Instead, just keep asking yourself, "What would make me feel better right now, until I get through this?" As long as you are not neglecting important responsibilities like work or your children, go easy on yourself during this period of healing.

Sherina says, "I ate a lot of chocolate bars and nachos and watched a lot of escapist movies while I was getting over my divorce with Shelley. Most of our friends seemed to side with her in the divorce because they were not poly, and they mistakenly blamed my having another relationship for the demise of the marriage. The reality of the situation was that Shelley and I just became more and more incompatible as our relationship went on. We were able to gloss over those differences for the first couple of years, but after seven years together, we were constantly fighting about housework, money, sex, and stupid shit like what to cook for dinner. Opening up the relationship was Shelley's idea, but her new lover dumped her after six months, and the fact that I had another lover was pretty irrelevant to our breakup. But she ended up with all our friends to hang out with, and I spent a lot of my time with my lover, Glenna. Luckily Glenna had been through a poly divorce herself, and she told me she spent three months doing nothing but going to work every day and then reading trashy novels every night, just to avoid thinking about the breakup. She was willing to sit in front of the TV with me and eat junk food and not expect too much from me. She understood that I just needed to zone out and distract myself from the pain. She told me as long as I could still go to work and bring home a paycheck so she wouldn't have to support both of us, I could veg out for a couple of months and I would get through it. She was right of course, and pretty soon I started going to the gym again, and re-planting my vegetable garden, which had died completely while I was too much of a mess to even water it. I felt like I was returning to the land of the living, and even some of the friends started calling and wanting to resume our friendship. They apologized for ignoring me but said they were worried about Shelley because she was all alone, and since I had Glenna they thought I would be okay. I realized that a poly divorce is also tough on the friends. Once the worst was over, they reached out to me again."

For Karen, losing her lover, Yassar, sent her into a spiral of depression. She was having trouble getting through the day at work without crying, and she couldn't sleep at night. She was always thinking about Yassar and feeling that he left her because she somehow wasn't good enough. She knew this was irrational, since their relationship had collapsed under the weight of the cultural differences between them, including religion, class, race, and a language barrier. Yassar had thought he could withstand the disapproval of his family, but he was racked with guilt about disappointing them by not marrying someone of his own religion and culture. In time, he started to withdraw from Karen, and eventually, he felt forced to end the relationship.

Karen's other lover, Jeffrey, happened to be out of town on a month-long trip when Yassar left her, so he wasn't available to provide comfort and distraction. Karen knew she needed a self-care program, so she went back to her previous therapist and learned some cognitive behavioral techniques to manage her depression more effectively. She started going swimming three times a week at the YMCA, since exercise had previously helped reduce her depression and insomnia. Her doctor prescribed a low dose of sleeping pills for a month, so she was able to get back on track with her sleep. She was gradually able to accept that there had been many obstacles to the success of her relationship with Yassar, and that most of these were out of her control. She stopped blaming herself for everything that went wrong in their relationship, and let go of some of the persistent self-criticism that had plagued her. By then, Jeffrey was back in town and suggested spending the weekend in bed together and ordering food. That turned out to be "just what the doctor ordered," as Karen puts it.

Bettye felt rejected and crushed by her husband leaving her for his much younger girlfriend. "I had suspected from the start that his insistence on opening up our marriage was just the first stage of abandoning me, and I don't think he really was poly," she say. "I was angry at being jerked around for a year while he fell in love with her, and then dumped me. I always felt like I was the reliable, responsible wife at home who he counted on to take care of the house, the yard, the dog, and to do our taxes. After all those years of playing that role, I had been thrown overboard for this 'shiny new toy.' I decided I needed to do something totally out of character to remind myself that I am a vibrant and beautiful woman. I had always loved biking and other sports, and before I got married I had done a few triathlons. So I took a six-month leave of absence from my job, and spent the first four months training for a serious bike trip across Australia. It gave me a goal and something to focus my time and energy on, instead of just feeling bad about myself and moping about my ex and his cute, young girlfriend. My confidence and my self-esteem really increased, and by the time I got to Australia for the bike trip, I really didn't even care about him anymore. I was having more fun than I had had in decades, and was becoming a person that I liked a whole lot more than the person I had been in the marriage. And it sure didn't hurt that I met a hunky, Aussie biker and had a passionate love affair at the end of my trip."

Brent had a similar approach to self-care. He had been living with his partner, Sampa, for nine years, and also had another girlfriend, Giara, who he had been involved with for four years. He had been in rock bands throughout his teens and 20s, but he gave it up because Sampa complained so much about him spending so many evenings at rehearsals and doing gigs. After 10 years, their relationship went down in flames due to her drinking problem and her running up their joint credit cards, leading to them both to declare bankruptcy. At first Brent literally felt suicidal, and could not imagine life without Sampa. Ending that relationship shook his foundation, and made him wonder if he could ever succeed in a committed, long-term relationship. Once they sold their house and he was living alone again, Brent started writing songs, connected with a few other musicians, and started playing some gigs around the city. He realized how much he had missed being part of a band and being on stage performing. He became convinced that he had given up too much of himself and his dreams in order to keep peace in his relationship, and decided that in any future relationship, he would not abandon his music.

Gay Men Have Been Leading the Way in Open Relationships

Harold is a 72-year-old gay man and a psychologist who provides guidance to his clients on navigating open relationships. He says, "The straight people are actually quite late to the party with this poly thing. Gay men have been practicing open relationships for a long time, in my case, personally, for over 50 years, and many of us are pretty good at it. Part of the reason for that is that we don't have the whole relationship-escalator baggage that the heterosexuals have, about how every relationship is supposed to lead to commitment, cohabiting, marriage, a house, kids, and a dog. Instead, we can allow each relationship to be what it naturally should be, and we have created pretty clear labels to help define that. For instance, a trick is someone you pick up at a bar or the baths or a park or cruising area and have (usually) anonymous sex with. A fuck-buddy is a good friend who you also have sex with, but the relationship is based primarily in friendship, not in romance. The friendship usually precedes the sexual relationship, and the friendship will continue long after the sex is over. A lover is someone you have a short, but very hot, fling with, like when you are on vacation or at a conference, or are staying somewhere for the summer or a semester abroad. A boyfriend is someone you are dating, either short-term or long-term, who may or may not become a serious relationship in the future. A husband is the person you live with and share finances with, the person you are planning on growing old with. And occasionally you might share other tricks or fuck-buddies with your husband, too."

Harold strongly advises clarifying early on what the status of each relationship is, so that no one is under any illusions, and no one will be disappointed later on. "Straight people seem to think it is terribly cruel to gently and gracefully let someone know that they are a fuck-buddy or a boyfriend rather than a candidate for husband status. But leading them on and creating false expectations is much worse than just telling them the truth. If there are limits and constraints on any relationship, the kindest thing you can do is give someone the whole truth so they can make an informed choice about whether to get involved or not. If they know what they are getting into, they can choose to opt out now if they don't like the situation, or they can sleep with you but not invest themselves in the relationship so they won't get their heart broken, or constantly be annoyed that you're not more available."

While many gay men may quibble over some of Harold's terms and definitions, there is a lot of consensus in the gay male community about different types of relationships and their specific role and status. As he says, "It doesn't really matter what labels you use for each relationship, as long as each person in the pool with you agrees on what that term means."

Harold has good advice about surviving a poly breakup: "Reach out to friends for support, ask them to include you in social activities, lunches, going out to clubs, and parties. Try not to rely too heavily on your other lovers to help you through this. They are probably really tired of hearing about this partner who dumped you, and they probably don't particularly want to spend their dates with you holding your hand while you cry about this other guy you are so in love with who has done you wrong."

Some poly people make the mistake of jumping back into dating new people when they are not really in any condition to start a new relationship. For some people, a few casual dates can be a lot of fun and help you feel desirable again when you are feeling rejected. However, you may not be thinking clearly, and it can be challenging to make good choices about who to date and what kind of relationship to have with them. And no one wants to feel like they are being used as a crutch while you are on the rebound, only to be dropped once you have recovered from the breakup and realized that you have nothing in common.

Pia says, "I had been with both of my partners for over 20 years, and then Rich dumped me for his other lover because she accidentally got pregnant and suddenly demanded monogamy. I had not done any dating for so long, I didn't have a clue about OKCupid or Tinder or any other way to meet people besides going to a party or bar. I got a dating app and suddenly people were asking me for dates. I was like the kid in the proverbial candy store, and got myself in a lot of trouble dating random people who were all wrong for me. I ended up hurting a few people by dating them once or twice and then not knowing how to call it off. I actually had to get help from my 23-year-old daughter to learn the new etiquette and how it's done nowadays. She taught me terms like 'ghosting' and, as she put it, 'how not be a douche, Mom.'"

CHAPTER TWELVE:

Grieve Your Losses and Learn Whatever Lessons You Can from This Relationship

This does *not* mean that you should wallow in self-loathing, or seethe in anger at your ex and dissect the relationship and its ending in excruciating detail. Most people already do way too much of this during and after a breakup. Obsessing about every painful incident and trying to place blame is, ultimately, futile and damaging to everyone involved.

Instead, it can be very useful to take a good hard look at the bigger picture of this relationship and learn as much as you can about yourself, your beliefs, your behavior, and your needs. First, think about what drew you into this relationship in the first place? What was it about this person and this relationship that was so compelling and so satisfying? What were you seeking in getting involved in this relationship? What made you stay in this relationship as long as you did? Think about which of your most important needs were met through this relationship, and what qualities and behaviors you loved about your partner. As difficult as it may be right now, try to cultivate some semblance of gratitude for the joy you experienced in this relationship, and the love and companionship you received. The pain you are going through now does not erase all the good things you experienced with your partner, and remembering that can help you get through this terribly bleak period.

Remember that a poly relationship that ends doesn't have to be viewed as a failure, because longevity is not the only proof of a successful relationship. It is not realistic to expect that every new relationship will last a lifetime, and losing some poly partners along the way is inevitable. There were probably a lot of wonderful experiences in this relationship, and it may be comforting to remind yourself that you received a lot more love and pleasure than pain.

Rachel says, "I was so depressed when Jenny left me that I literally forgot about the 10 years of happiness we had. I was trashing her all over the community, and I was convinced our entire relationship was a sham. One of my friends got sick of my ranting and of having to defend Jenny, who was also her friend. She grabbed my phone from me and started scrolling through all the photos: Jenny and me in Hawaii backpacking, Jenny and me doing volunteer work mentoring queer youth, Jenny and me marching in the Gay Pride Parade, Jenny and me riding our bikes in the AIDS Life Cycle ride together, looking ridiculous in shorts and matching Lesbian Avengers T-shirts and our hairy legs! And most hilarious of all, Jenny and I being freaking bridesmaids in high heels and gowns at our gay male friends' very fancy wedding. Then my friend literally slaps me and yells, 'You should be so glad you were so happy together and had such a great life together, you moron! Lots of people never get that lucky!' I sheepishly had to admit that that dumbass cliché is true—that it *is* better to have loved and lost than to not have loved at all. A decade of a great relationship totally outweighed the six months of fighting and misery before we broke up, and the three months I had spent recovering. What would I do without my friends to kick my ass when I am being such an idiot?"

Remembering the gifts she received in her relationship allowed Rachel to grieve her losses and let go of her anger. She was still sad and lonely for another month while she moved through her grieving process, but she could feel herself becoming more accepting of the new reality rather than raging against the unfairness of it and seeing herself as a victim.

It can be hard to be objective about anything when you are crushed by a painful breakup. But try to make a realistic assessment about whether your ex-partner had good relationships skills in general, and whether they were an ideal relationship partner for *you* in particular. As Jane says, "I kept trying to blame Liz for everything that was wrong with our relationship and make her the villain of the story. It was very hard to admit that, actually, she was a great person and had excellent relationship skills. This was what made me love her so much! However, she was just all wrong for me, and everyone else had been telling me that for years. My friends all loved her and agreed she was a fantastic person, but they could see that we were on a collision course. She liked to party, take psychedelics, have lots of casual sex and threesomes with other women, and travel around the world without even having a permanent home anywhere. She did website design remotely, so she could work while traveling, and finance her nomadic lifestyle comfortably. I have a nine-to-five job, I like routine and stability, and I find travel very stressful. I don't enjoy casual sex, and I'm terrified of group sex."

Because they had such a fantastic intellectual rapport and great sexual chemistry, Jane and Liz thought that this was enough for a successful relationship. But eventually their differences created so much conflict that it seemed like they were constantly fighting. Liz insisted on going on a two-month trip and Jane felt abandoned, but she couldn't take any more time off work to travel with Liz. She demanded that Liz not have sex with other women while on the trip, and Liz refused, ultimately ending the relationship. Jane eventually realized that she was really asking Liz to be a different person than she actually was. She was twisting herself into a pretzel trying to embrace a lifestyle of travel and partying that did not suit her temperament and was not financially realistic for her.

"I finally admitted that great sex and feeling connected on an intellectual level are both very important to me, but that I also need a partner who has much more in common with me," she says. "I know now that any life partner needs to be compatible with me in all three of those ways." Jane eventually fell in love with another woman, who was much more aligned with her values and lifestyle. Catalina is a writer, and she and Jane have great conversations about literature and art. They live together and spend their free time going to museums and poetry readings. They are more sexually and emotionally compatible because they both want a primary relationship that is not monogamous, but where each of them can have outside relationships that are secondary and ongoing. And Jane has what she jokingly calls her "bonus" lover—when Liz is in town, they spend time together and often have sex, with Catalina's blessing.

Clio learned an even more humbling lesson from his breakup with Hazel—that his own relationship skills needed work in order to have a healthy polyamorous relationship.

"Like most people going through a horrible breakup, I was furious with Hazel for leaving me, and blamed her for giving up on our beautiful love," he says. "I told myself she was just too needy and just couldn't handle polyamory. She always freaked out when I would get involved with other women. I needed a lot of freedom, and did not want to negotiate with her about my outside relationships or have any limits. I always told her to stop trying to control me, but she felt I didn't care about her, and that my expectations were unrealistic. After five years, she finally broke up with me. She said I claimed I wanted a committed relationship, but at the same time I wanted to behave exactly the same as if I was single. I thought she was just a drama queen and that she needed to get over being so possessive."

However, when Clio went to a poly support group, he got feedback from many people in the group that very few women would have been happy with his behavior or attitudes. He says, "Hazel was working really hard to manage her jealousy, and to give me more and more freedom as she felt more secure in the relationship. But I was not giving her enough appreciation or acknowledgement of how much she was doing. Instead, I just kept pushing the envelope and having more outside relationships." One man in the support group said, "Dude, your sense of entitlement is off the charts! If I had even half the freedom in my marriage that you did in your relationship with Hazel, I would be on my knees thanking my wife for being so flexible." A woman in the group empathized with Clio, saying, "I lost two marriages because I was so stubborn in doing whatever I wanted, and I didn't care how much it hurt my husbands. I believed that their feelings were their problem and that they should learn to be happy with a sexually liberated wife. I was callous about their pain, and refused to compromise. And I paid a steep price for it. After losing both husbands, I finally 'got it' that in a committed relationship, everyone has to feel safe and loved, and that means I have to give my partners the support they need, and respect their hard limits."

Getting that reality check helped Clio understand that poly relationships require a lot of give and take. "Before this, I thought that my version of polyamory was 'the one true path,' and I did not feel flexible about making compromises," he says. "I thought that in order to be true to myself, I couldn't accept any restrictions. I realize now that each person has their own unique set of needs and limits, and that I need to listen and work with a partner to come to agreements that work for both of us."

Hazel had her own steep learning curve, both in the relationship with Clio and in the aftermath of their breakup. She says, "During the whole relationship, I blamed Clio for never giving me enough time, attention, and primacy. But I was at least as responsible as he was for all that pain, because Clio told me on our very first date that he wanted relationship anarchy and *no* rules. He was very honest with me and I should have listened! He said he needed 'a low-maintenance partner who never got jealous and wasn't needy.' I should have been smart enough to know right then that he was *all* wrong for me! I need to be part of a couple, and he did not want to be in a couple, he wanted to be a free agent. If I had had any sense at all, I would have fled immediately! But I felt such an intense connection with him that I tried to accept the relationship on his terms. I spent five years trying to be okay with him sleeping with every attractive woman who crossed his path, and doing a disappearing act whenever he was having NRE with a new lover. I went to therapy to try to change myself, and I did make great progress in dramatically reducing my jealousy and becoming much more independent and less reactive every time he developed a new crush. However, the more self-sufficient I became, the less I wanted to be in this relationship. I no longer felt needy and I knew I would be better off without him."

Hazel learned that she wanted a more hierarchical model of polyamory, where she could count on being prioritized by her partner, so as she started dating again, she was much more honest with potential partners about her needs. "Clio had constantly guilt-tripped me into thinking my needs didn't matter, and I was never allowed to ask for anything. He even told me that I was weak and that I wasn't a 'real feminist' because I would get insecure and want reassurance," she says. "I now know that these are just my basic needs for security and predictability in a relationship. Instead of feeling bad about myself, or blaming him, I just need to find an appropriate partner who shares my vision of a poly relationship. Knowing who I am and what I want, and communicating that to any potential partner, makes me a much better relationship partner now."

Simon struggled through two poly breakups in a row, before finally succeeding on his third try. In his first poly relationship, he fell in love with a woman who eventually realized she needed a monogamous relationship. Simon and Minna fought for years, with her constantly demanding more time and commitment and sabotaging any outside relationships he tried to pursue. She broke up with him when he refused to give in to her demand that he break up with another lover. Then he swung from one extreme to the other when he fell in love with Larissa, who had a demanding career, a teenage son at home, and two other casual sexual partners. He reasoned that she was too busy and too committed to be as possessive of his time and loyalty as Minna had been, and he was right about that.

However, Larissa guarded her time, her autonomy, and her privacy fiercely, and was only available to see him once a week for dinner and sex, and was not open to very much emotional intimacy and connection. Simon felt lonely and unsatisfied with the amount of love and companionship she was willing or able to provide. He was embarrassed to find himself behaving exactly like Minna had, pleading for more time and attention, wanting more commitment and intimacy from Larissa. She stood her ground and insisted that this was a much as she could offer him, that her child and her job had to take priority. The relationship fizzled out rapidly, leaving Simon feeling like a failure at polyamory. He despaired of ever finding a partner who was willing and able to meet his needs for love and companionship without being too possessive or insisting on monogamy.

Through attending a poly discussion group and going to a poly-friendly therapist, Simon became more comfortable with himself and found a "middle-ground approach" to open relationships. He realized that after his breakup with Minna, he was so eager to have more freedom that he had accidentally "over-corrected" and chosen someone who was emotionally unavailable and too busy for a relationship. He would need to search for a woman who really wanted love and commitment, but who also had experience with polyamory, had actively chosen that path of relationship, and had a good skill set to manage jealousy. Simon realized that he would probably have to compromise in some areas.

For instance, he might have to agree to more limits on his outside relationships in order to receive a higher level of commitment and emotional intimacy from a partner. Or he might need to accept less time and security in a relationship in order to have total freedom and no rules about his other relationships. His therapist reminded him that in any relationship, romantic or otherwise, both people agree to give up some fraction of their independence in order to have the benefits that interpersonal relationships offer. In all relationships, including those with family members and platonic friends, we choose to consistently commit time and energy, and to be there for others in times of need, even if it is inconvenient or difficult. In exchange, we receive closeness, love, support, and companionship. In a romantic or sexual relationship, we make an informed decision that the benefits of the relationship are so precious to us that we are voluntarily choosing to give up some of the benefits of being single and doing whatever we want. Simon realized that he had been seeing only the "cost," and was feeling victimized by any limits or agreements requested by a partner. He was feeling coerced rather than feeling at choice to negotiate any boundaries.

For Johnny, grieving the end of his relationship with Eleanor brought up his very painful past. He realized that the hardest thing about the breakup was that he had never felt loved and accepted by anyone in his entire life before his relationship with Eleanor. He had been physically abused by his father and rejected by his mother because he was transgender. Johnny escaped by running away from home at age 15 and becoming a sex worker on the streets of New York City. Ten years later, he was addicted to speed, lonely, and frightened before he became involved with Eleanor and felt safe and loved for the first time in his life. However, getting clean and sober, starting hormone therapy, and having surgeries related to his gender transition all took a toll on their relationship. Neither he nor Eleanor had prior experience being poly, and they both made some mistakes in neglecting their relationship while in the throes of NRE in their outside relationships. Johnny went into a deep depression after being dumped by his new girlfriend, who decided she did not want to be involved with a trans-masculine person, and Eleanor was so exhausted by that point that she ended their relationship. Johnny went into therapy and discovered that he had to truly grieve his family's rejection before he could really grieve the loss of his relationship with Eleanor. Because Eleanor had given him such unconditional love, he had come to believe he truly deserved love, and that he was worthy of a healthy and happy relationship. And even though the relationship had ended, it had given him the confidence to believe he would be loved again in the future. These were the real gifts of the relationship—he knew what it was like to be truly loved and he had learned how to be a good partner in a loving relationship. As horrible as the breakup was, understanding its real and lasting benefits allowed Johnny to eventually make peace with losing the relationship.

It is normal to experience sadness and a bruised ego after any breakup. However, an honest appraisal of the relationship and the causes of its demise can be very educational, and is likely to help you in any future relationships. Learn what you can from what happened in a relationship and be willing to apply that wisdom when you feel ready to love again.

CHAPTER THIRTEEN:

Sustaining Your Other Relationship(s) Throughout the Breakup

The majority of polyamorous people going through a breakup have at least one other partner, and this can be very comforting and supportive during this hellish time. However, it can also be very difficult, because other relationships require your energy and attention at a time when you are at your worst. When you have multiple partners, and one of them leaves you, you still have the responsibility to maintain and sustain the remaining relationship(s). This can be extremely challenging, because it is very difficult to mourn the ending of a relationship and at the same time remain present and available for your remaining partner or partners.

Lennie says, "In my past, I was in a monogamous relationship living with Jessica, and when she dumped me, I went to work on autopilot and somehow managed to avoid getting fired. I went from work to a sports bar every night and drank beer and watched football. I didn't talk to anyone and didn't have any responsibility towards anyone. But this time, I was in a poly relationship living with Angelica, and had been dating Stacy for two years. Stacy had been expressing some dissatisfaction about our relationship because she wanted to live together. Suddenly she broke up with me. It seemed like it was out of nowhere, but in retrospect I can see she was gradually deciding she wanted a relationship where she could live with someone and be the alpha female. I was in a state of shock, and on top of that, I had no idea how to go through a poly breakup. I tried talking to Angelica about it, but she really didn't want to console me every night about how much I missed Stacy, and yeah, I get that. I couldn't go to the sports bar and drink every night, because my partner expected and deserved my time and attention. I was completely unavailable for a relationship, as I was obsessed with, 'what did I do wrong and how could I fix things with Stacy.' I was so irrational that I even wondered if I should leave Angelica and offer to move in with Stacy, even though I knew that made no sense and would never work."

It often creates hurt, anger, and insecurity for a remaining partner to see just how upset their partner is about losing another partner. A common response from the existing partner is "What am I, chopped liver?" It is shocking to see a partner totally falling apart and be devastated by the departure of the other partner. The message that the remaining partner may believe they are receiving is that the other relationship was much more important than they are, even though that is usually not true. When you have just experienced a painful loss, you are focused on that other partner because you are trying to process your grief and get over it. The intensity of that pain can activate the remaining partner's insecurities about themselves and the relationship. They may suspect that you don't love them or want them, because you are experiencing so much longing for the other person, who is no longer available. And because you are probably talking incessantly about the breakup, the remaining partner may feel like you are so preoccupied with the other person's departure that you are completely uninterested in them.

One long-suffering partner reports feeling like "I'm still here, so why aren't you happy with me?" Another says, "I've been so loyal and stood by you through all the shenanigans with your girlfriend! I hung in there through the NRE stage when you neglected me, while spending our joint money buying her flowers and taking her on romantic dates. I stayed with you through the ups and downs with this chick for over five years. I held your hand through her breaking up with you and getting back together three times. And now she ends it for good, and you've spent the last four months crying over her and trying to win her back, and totally ignoring my existence."

When going through a breakup you are often in no condition to actually connect with your remaining partner, because you feel so depressed and confused over losing the other partner. As a result, you are inadvertently creating the impression that this other lover was much more important to you than you let on while the relationship existed.

Luigi tried to be what he calls "a good poly role model" by supporting Sylvia through a bruising breakup with her girlfriend, Elsa. He cooked her favorite meals, took her out for a spa day with a massage and a manicure, and tried to be endlessly sympathetic to her tales of woe about "the girl who got away." After a few months of this, he acknowledged that it was starting to become tedious, saying he felt more like her therapist than her lover. Then Sylvia forgot to show up at his birthday party because she was having what she described as "major dyke drama," processing over the phone with Elsa about their breakup. He felt so hurt that he worried that maybe she had lied about her relationship with Elsa being secondary, and accused her of loving Elsa more than him. "If you want her so badly, and I'm so unimportant, maybe we should split up."

This was the wake-up call that shocked Sylvia out of what she calls "my narcissistic wallow." She says, "Suddenly I realized that if I didn't get my head out of my ass, I was going to lose Luigi. I was so in love with him, but I had been taking him for granted to some extent because I was so blown out of the water by Elsa leaving me. She was the first woman I had ever been involved with, and loving a woman was such an incredible experience that I didn't know if I could recover from losing her. I was horrified that my self-centered behavior was hurting Luigi, and that snapped me back into reality and to fully participating in my relationship with him again."

Brigit had two committed relationships, and reports a similar experience. Because she had been with Jason for 10 years, and Brian for six years, Brian felt that Jason "had seniority" and was more important, even though Brigit was deeply in love with both partners. She says, "Brian broke up with me because he never felt equal and wanted me to somehow prove he was just as important as Jason, and no matter what I did, it was never enough. We all lived together as a triad, we had joint bank accounts and credit cards, all our names were on the lease for the apartment, we owned cars together. I went on a vacation with both of them together once a year, and took short trips with each of them separately every year."

She was shocked and distraught over Brian leaving her, and kept thinking he would change his mind. He got his own apartment and would barely talk to her. She was pleading to see him and have some kind of friendship with him. He was very withdrawn, and this sent her into a spiral of sadness and self-doubt. She lost confidence in herself and her ability to have healthy relationships, and her self-esteem plummeted. She says, "Jason tried to be supportive, but my desperation and self-hatred were not exactly attractive, and certainly did not inspire romantic feelings on his part. Luckily, his long-term girlfriend, Tamara, lived nearby, and she was really giving him a lot of love and attention and support. Ironically, it was the first time I really experienced true compersion, probably because it was so obvious that I was benefiting from her relationship with Jason. She was essentially doing my job, as well as her own, in this relationship, and I was truly grateful to her because she was literally keeping my relationship with Jason afloat. She would even send healthy casseroles and fresh salads home with him since I was incapable of cooking or even shopping for food. If it wasn't for Tamara meeting all of Jason's relationship needs during that hellish several months, I probably would have lost him, too, since I was really not capable of being a good relationship partner. In fact, because they were spending so much time together, their relationship intensified in a very positive way. Once the worst of my breakup blues was over and I felt recovered, we asked Tamara to move in with us, and we have all been pretty happy since then. I still regret losing Brian, but now he is involved in a monogamous relationship, which I can see is making him happy, and he and I have finally been able to become friends."

Reginald explains that he found it too overwhelming to manage the ongoing demands of his wife, Jezanna, at the same time as he was reeling from losing his lover, Rupert. Rupert ended their four-year relationship because he married his other partner, Benjamin, and they decided to become monogamous. "I tried to be there for Jezanna because she had always been insecure about my bisexuality, and my relationship with Rupert tapped into her fears that I was really gay," Reginald says. "But as much as I tried to reassure her of my love and commitment, I was feeling so depleted by the breakup that I had very little to give her. She could tell I was distant and distracted, and she needed even more of my time and attention than usual, right at the time my gas tank was totally empty. So, not only was I in mourning over a lost love, on top of that I had a resentful, hurt wife demanding proof of my devotion to her."

Reginald joined a support group for poly men, which helped him talk through his grief and sadness. He started working out at the gym because he knew it would help him manage his anxiety and stop obsessing over Rupert. He felt more stable and started to feel more energized. He encouraged Jezanna to get support from their poly friends, which helped her feel more secure about their relationship. He was gradually able to give Jezanna more attention and love, and she started to relax and feel safer, saying "You're back to your old self again!"

Be Cautious About Making a Remaining Secondary Relationship into a Primary Relationship

There is sometimes another "poly wrinkle" when a primary relationship ends, and an outside or secondary relationship still exists. Often the secondary partner is initially thrilled because they now believe they will have the opportunity to develop a primary relationship with their partner. However, they are often quite disappointed that their suddenly available partner is not really available for that, and in fact is so depressed and unstable that they can barely provide the same amount of time and commitment they were giving to them before the breakup.

After Brent and Sampa split up, Brent and Giara continued in a loving sexual and romantic relationship. However, they both knew that their relationship worked best as what she called "a somewhat-secondary thing." They were not really compatible as primary partners or living together, as they had very different values and life plans. Giara was 10 years younger than Brent, and wanted to settle down and raise a family, which was not on Brent's agenda at all. He enjoyed the freedom of being "single," while having sex and companionship. He gave Giara his blessing to keep looking for a husband, and even introduced her to a few of his younger male friends who had expressed a strong desire to have children. Brent expressed a lot of gratitude to Giara for giving him so much love and support to get through what he called "the worst year of my life," and he was committed to helping her find happiness in her life. He told her, "I know I'm not Mr. Right, for you, I'm just Mr. Right Now, but that's okay, since you can date me and still look for him." A few years later, she found "the love of her life," and got married. Her husband wanted monogamy while they were getting pregnant and during the first years of childrearing, so she and Brent split up as lovers, but remained close friends.

Brent and Giara's story had a happy ending, even though they did not end up together as a couple. This is because when Brent and Sampa broke up, he resisted the temptation to "replace" her with Giara as his primary partner. Both Brent and Giara knew that this would end in disaster, as they had such different needs, especially around having children.

Many such tales do not end well, because when a primary relationship ends, there is a tendency to assume that any secondary relationship should now become primary. This may work if a partner were designated as secondary *only* because the original couple had chosen the primary/ secondary model of polyamory, and there is a high level of compatibility between these two people on most key relationship issues. Allowing a secondary relationship to evolve into a primary relationship usually requires being strongly aligned sexually, emotionally, intellectually, domestically, financially, and socially.

Unfortunately, many people fail to consider whether they are well-matched in these important arenas before deciding to shift to a much higher level of commitment, such as moving in together, getting married, or becoming pregnant. The fatal flaw is assuming that your track record of success in this secondary relationship is a strong predictor of its future success as a primary relationship. The structure, demands, and expectations in a primary relationship are much different. Many people are blissfully happy spending one night a week with their smart, amazing lover, and having the occasional weekend trip with them. Or they love the intense intellectual connection or emotional intimacy they share. Perhaps they very successfully work together as friends and lovers, for a political cause, or they are in a band together. But they are often quite distressed to discover serious problems crop up when they start spending more time together, or try to share living space or a bank account.

Amelia explains, "When Dennison and I were living together, we were great roommates, had similar values about work and money, and both kept the house at the same level of cleanliness. We really enjoyed each other's company and had an intense emotional connection. Unfortunately, we never had great chemistry, and our sex life was pretty routine and infrequent. We thought being poly would rescue our sex life, but instead we both fell in love with our outside lovers because we had such great sex with them. We had an amicable breakup, because our relationship had become pretty platonic, so neither of us was crushed by admitting we were no longer in love. However, we both made the mistake of moving in with our respective lovers almost immediately, and within six months both of those relationships imploded. We were blindsided and terribly embarrassed that we were both having another breakup! Upon further reflection, we had to admit that all those other relationships had going was sex, romance, and a few shared activities like tennis and dancing. In fact, each of us had little else in common with our partner and we were incompatible to live together because we did not have a lot of shared values and life goals. Ironically, while Dennison and I were together as a couple, all those basic needs of companionship and compatibility were being met at home, and the outside relationships could happily get by on just sex and fun. Once we split up, we needed more from them, and those relationships just couldn't provide it."

Many secondary relationships are initially defined this way because at least one of the people in the relationship already has a primary relationship. As a result, one or both people in that relationship may assume that the secondary label is just situational, rather than being based on any assessment of how compatible these two people would be for a life partnership.

Candice says, "When I got involved with Penny, she knew that Beatriz was my life partner." As Penny puts it, "I knew that slot was filled, and the only position available was as a very part-time lover. I was really looking for a wife, and

I thought Candice would be perfect for me if she was not already living with someone. But when Beatriz moved to Detroit to go to medical school, Candice couldn't find a job there, so she stayed in Chicago, where she already had a good job. After a year, the stress of a long-distance relationship on top of medical school took its toll, and they split up."

Penny thought Candice was now available as a full-time partner, and proposed marriage. Candice was distraught over the breakup with Beatriz, and was certainly not ready to jump into marriage with anyone. And she did not feel that she and Penny had enough compatibility or similar enough lifestyles to live together. For Candice, her priorities were working hard, making a good income, and saving for retirement. But Penny worked at a low-wage job and spent all her earnings on nice clothes and vacations, which were much more satisfying and valuable to her than financial security. In addition, Penny was very politically active in left-wing LGBT organizations, while Candice felt these groups were much too aggressive and "in your face," and favored assimilating into the larger straight, mainstream community. Candice felt convinced that these differences were manageable in a secondary relationship, but would become deal-breakers if they moved in together and tried to have a life together. Penny was crushed by what she experienced as a complete rejection, saying, "So I'm good enough for sex and having a good time, but I'm not good enough for a real relationship?" Often, a relationship is designated as secondary for a good reason, which usually means there is at least one area of incompatibility that would make a primary relationship difficult to sustain.

Sandra says, "Be careful what you wish for! I always thought I would be in heaven if Aja and Ruth divorced! Their marriage always got priority. And even though Aja always assured me that he loved me just as much, he lived with her and their marriage prevented me from having a more committed relationship with him. So when they split up, I thought he would move in with me full-time, and we could get married. However, he was totally paralyzed over the divorce, obsessing about how their marriage had failed, going over everything that happened and trying to figure out what he could have done differently to save his marriage. Since she had moved out, he clung to the house as the only remaining security and continuity in his life, and did not want to move in with me. He needed a lot of time to himself, and when we did have dates, he was just a mess and could not really give me his full attention. I had to remind him to eat meals and take showers. And he was constantly on the phone with Ruth bickering over the divorce and trying to reach a financial settlement. Of course Ruth blamed me for somehow wrecking their marriage even though they were poly long before he met me, and she also had a boyfriend. To put it mildly, the romantic bliss I had expected when they divorced did not materialize."

Be Honest with Your Remaining Partner(s) about Your Impaired Capacity

Sitting down and honestly talking to your partner can go a long way towards making them an ally in the healing process. Explain to them that you are doing your best to struggle through this breakup with your other partner. Be frank about the fact that you are not at your best right now, and that for a while a least, you are unable to be emotionally available enough to meet their needs. Thank them for their love, patience, and support during this very painful time, and reassure them that you will find your way through it as quickly as possible. Remind them that you both share the same goal: for life to get back to normal as soon as humanly possible, and that with their help, you will get there sooner. Ask them how they feel about the situation, and try not to be defensive if they seem critical or express frustrations with you. Listening to their feelings and concerns right now is very important, even if you feel you have little energy to try to do better at the moment. You are not promising any spectacular changes, just hearing what they're going through right now and validating their feelings. Many people in their situation report feeling ignored and neglected while a partner is depressed and distracted with a breakup, so being as good of a listener as possible right now can really make your partner feel loved and understood. Ask them whether they need anything specific from you, even if you are not sure you can provide it right now.

Shizuko was flattened by her breakup with Manny, even though she was the one who broke up with him after he relapsed into opiate addiction and lost his job as a result. She felt overwhelmed by her job, house, her partner, Ron, and helping to care for her elderly father, who had recently had a stroke. She felt that for the time being, she could not keep up with everything. She felt panicked about disappointing Ron, slacking off work, or letting everyone down.

She considered temporarily cutting back on her work hours as a bartender and taking a cut in pay, to relieve the pressure and to give her more time and energy to manage everything else. However, she was afraid Ron would be angry that she was not pulling her weight financially, so she asked him to share his personal hierarchy of what was most important to him. "If I only work 30 hours a week instead of 40, I'll have more time and energy for our relationship, be able to keep up with the housework and cooking, and continue helping Mom with my father every weekend," she said. "Would you be upset if I don't work full-time for the next couple of months?" Ron said they were doing okay financially, so it was fine for her to work less, and that her being able to be more present in their relationship was much more important to him. "We can get by on less money for a while, but I don't think I can survive feeling ignored and alone for much longer while you hide in the spare bedroom playing video games and crying all night. And maybe you could ask one of your brothers to help take care of your dad for one weekend this month, so we can get out of town," he said.

Shizuko was relieved that Ron was fine with her working less, and suddenly everything seemed a lot more manageable. Her brother helped with her father's care, and she and Ron drove up north for a weekend of wine tasting, art galleries, and lots of sex at a secluded cottage. Ron was thrilled that she was smiling again and really connecting with him. There was an additional perk to her working less—because she worked at the bar until 2 AM three nights a week, working one less shift meant they had an extra evening together every week. They started going out to movies and to see bands more often, and they had sex more often because she was home in the evening more.

Erik felt so numb and sad after Jocelyn broke up with him that he withdrew from his wife, Rosalie. The more Rosalie pleaded with him for affection and lovemaking, the more pressured he felt. He explained that it was really difficult for him have sex right now, because it required more emotional intimacy than he could handle while feeling so rotten about himself. Rosalie said she could live without sex for a while, but "I'm going to shrivel up and die if you won't hold me and give me some affection." As soon as the expectation of sex was removed from the equation, Erik felt much more able to cuddle in bed with her, kissing her and sometimes stroking her breasts and gently undressing her. She was thrilled, saying "This is so romantic! It's like when we were first dating!" A few times he got sad and weepy and needed to withdraw, but most nights they were loving and affectionate, and before long they were able to have sex again pretty frequently.

The take home message is to communicate *more* rather than less when you are going through a painful poly breakup. Many people have expressed reluctance to talk to their remaining partner about what they are going through out of fear that they won't be capable of providing what their partner needs from them or fear that they will feel even worse for having "failed" their partner. Or they fear asking their partner to share their experience and feelings about the breakup, because this seems like giving their partner an open invitation to criticize or yell at them. It's certainly true that these conversations can be awkward and painful. However, most people report relief that both parties have gotten their feelings, resentments, and fears out in the open, and this usually leads to feeling closer and more emotionally connected again. Often, some simple but useful problem solving ideas come out of the discussion, which can make both partners feel much better.

CHAPTER FOURTEEN:

Handling the Public Relations of a Poly Breakup

Many people going through the end of an open relationship have been unpleasantly surprised by the intense reactions of friends, family, coworkers, and neighbors. Because monogamy is the culturally approved norm, most people live their polyamorous lives with a "siege mentality," constantly having to justify themselves and their relationships to everyone around them.

As Bennie puts it, "Whether we like it or not, most people believe poly relationships can't work, or that they shouldn't work. So it feels like everyone is just waiting for us to fail so they can say, 'See, I just knew that poly thing would blow up in your face!'" Janine had a similar experience with her friends and family. She says, "At the same time I was distraught over losing the love of my life, I had to do a ton of 'damage control' to manage a public relations disaster as well."

Valerie says, "My mother told me over and over again that my husband would leave me because I was 'sleeping around,' as she put it. So when our marriage *did* end, even though our divorce had nothing to do with polyamory, she couldn't wait to pounce on me and remind me that she had predicted this! She obviously felt vindicated."

Justin says, "I had been married and divorced twice, and both relationships were strictly monogamous. No one ever blamed either of those breakups on monogamy. And everyone was so sympathetic when I was going through a divorce, asking me out to dinner, calling to see how I'm doing, and sending me friendly emails and cat videos to cheer me up. Some of my friends were even trying to set me up on dates with new women. Then I had a poly relationship that lasted twice as long as either of my marriages, and when we split up everyone blamed it on the fact that we weren't monogamous. No one was supportive or caring, and a few people I had thought were my friends even told me I got what I deserved for trying to have two girlfriends. One female friend said she was 'so glad that at least *one* of those women had enough self-respect to kick you to the curb.'"

Lack of data makes it impossible to hazard an educated guess about whether polyamorous relationships are any more likely to end than monogamous relationships. However, most people going through the demise of an open relationship find themselves and their relationships being vilified, even by their closest friends.

Catherine's best friend sighed and said, "Well, I tried to be supportive because you claimed you were poly, but I knew all along that could never work! What were you thinking?" Catherine felt crushed by her friend's judgment, right when she desperately needed support. "I was feeling so vulnerable, and suddenly I had to defend myself and my relationship orientation," she says. "And my best friend and I are both lesbians, so I asked her, 'How would *you* feel if a straight friend told you that a recent breakup was all because you was gay, and that you should marry a man instead!' She was indignant and said it's not the same thing at all, but I said that being poly is my sexual orientation just as much as being gay."

Susan says, "I was even handed that old chestnut I used to hear from people 30 years ago when I came out as bisexual: 'You just want to have your cake and eat it, too!' I thought I would never hear that idiotic nonsense again, but after my girlfriend split up with me, a number of my straight friends resurrected that old line to let me know that they did not approve of polyamory, that I deserved to fail, and that, apparently, they were happy my relationship ended."

When Geo told his sister that his girlfriend had left him because she and his wife did not get along very well, his sister responded with, "Thank goodness she came to her senses while she's still young enough to find a husband and have children. You were ruining her life by stringing her along when you could never marry her." Geo was shocked to hear his relationship being seen through such a distorted lens. "My girlfriend was polyamorous and had another long-term partner, and she certainly didn't want to marry me. She didn't leave me because we were polyamorous. People just jump to crazy conclusions based on their monogamous worldview, rather than the facts of the situation," he says.

While no one enjoys facing hostile judgment from loved ones for their relationship choices, it is especially difficult during such a painful experience of loss and grief. Amber recalled previous breakups where her three "gal pals" closed ranks behind her as loyal supporters, talking trash about her exes and saying, "He's not worth it, girlfriend!" and "He never deserved you, honey!" Then, she was in an open relationship for five years. Her boyfriend moved to another city with his live-in partner because the partner's company transferred her to a different office. He and Amber eventually decided to break up due to the strain of trying to maintain a long-distance relationship. This time, all three of her friends defended the boyfriend. They said, "What did you expect? He was with her for a year longer than with you," and, "You should have known better than to get involved with a guy who already had a girlfriend. He's probably going to marry her, couldn't you see he's committed to her, not to you?" A few of Amber's cousins heard about the breakup through a mutual friend's Facebook post, and suddenly she was getting messages from distant relatives around the country chastising her for "dating a married man," (which wasn't even true) and offering ridiculous advice including, "You should stay out of the street and keep your nose clean." This sent Amber into a spiral of humiliation and depression. "People who barely knew me were publicly shaming me without even really knowing anything about my relationship," she says.

In their 2014 book, *More Than Two,* Eve Rickert and Franklin Veaux remind us, "Most of us have deeply internalized messages about what's okay in relationships. Polyamory requires us to uproot and discard many of those messages. This becomes a lot harder if the people we turn to for support reinforce those messages whenever we confide in them."

On the topic of breakups they say, "If the members of the couple are primarily tapped into monogamous culture, the story that will get traction will be the standard cheating narrative. That will be doubly true if it appears that one person left their partner for someone else…The shaming this can entail can be extremely destructive if you have even a trace of those monogamous scripts left in your own internal self-evaluation process."

Rickert and Veaux stress the importance of having polyamorous friends and being part of an organized poly community, including discussion groups, poly social events, and staying connected to online poly networks. This helps to counteract the negative reactions of monogamously oriented friends and family members who may not understand your relationships and the pain and loss you are experiencing.

Managing the public relations aspect of a poly breakup can be challenging and draining. Carl says, "It's almost like you're speaking a different language than everyone else. So no matter what you say, they assume the breakup is your own fault because you were crazy enough to try this open relationship thing." So how can you cope with this backlash and effectively communicate with loved ones and others in your life?

Mark and Tricia crafted a carefully worded email, which they sent out to their close friends and family members, saying that they had decided to separate. They explained that they had enjoyed 25 years of happiness together, and raised two great kids who were now in college. They had been growing apart for the past few years, and while they still loved each other, they both believed that they would be happier living separately, and eventually divorcing. They made a point of stating clearly that they had been polyamorous through their entire marriage, and that this had not been a factor in their decision to separate. They also said that they intended to continue to be close friends and to both be there for their children. They ended with, "We ask all of you to be understanding and compassionate, and to be there for both of us as we take the next steps. We need your love and support at this challenging time of our lives." Many people who received the email did not respond at all. However, those that did reply responded with kindness and care, sending emails or calling with reassurance that they would stand by them.

One friend later apologized to Tricia for not responding to her email. She said, "I felt awkward and did not know what to say. A lot of other couples I knew that have divorced hated each other and spent years in divorce court fighting over the house, the bank accounts, and custody of the kids. That seemed normal! I actually didn't know how to respond to a couple who were divorcing and being so civilized about it; you were presenting yourselves as friends and not trashing each other." Tricia suspects that many others did not respond to their email for similar reasons. "Most people are simply stymied for an appropriate response when two people are separating, but there is no villain to blame and no victim to rally behind," she says.

Mark adds, "I feel convinced that if we had *not* sent out that email, we would have gotten a lot of calls from people assuming that one of our other partners had caused the divorce, or that our being polyamorous was to blame. My other girlfriend, Wenda, jokingly called it 'your pre-emptive strike,' and Tricia's boyfriend referred to it as 'your divorce press release.' They both agreed that putting the facts out there right away prevented any rumors from flying around and helped people understand and respond in a caring manner. Wenda says she had been worried that everyone would somehow blame her for breaking up a family, when in fact I'm in a committed partnership with someone else and our relationship is very secondary." Wenda adds, "Mark was surprised I would even be concerned about that, but people are so eager to jump on 'the other woman' when a divorce happens, they just assume it must be your fault. So I was so relieved that he and Tricia were setting the record straight before anyone could start spinning these imaginary soap-opera scenarios, and trashing me on social media."

David and Jenna decided to divorce after 25 years together. They were members of a progressive synagogue in New York, and asked the rabbi (now retired) who had presided over their wedding to facilitate an "uncoupling" ritual. They had been monogamous for many years and had struggled for several years after Jenna started a relationship with another man. Despite much effort, David was not able to accept this significant change in their marriage, saying, "This is not what I want, and it's completely different than what I signed up for." The rabbi helped them create an appropriate ritual that honored their decades-long partnership. Their friends and some of their family members attended the ceremony to support them. The last part of the ritual involved them each expressing their love and acknowledging that they were not compatible to continue together. They thanked each other for the "20 great years" they had together before issues arose. David told Jenna that he accepted that she was polyamorous, and she told him that she accepted that he needed an exclusive relationship. As a result, they agreed to let go of each other and their marriage. They both turned to their friends and family members and asked for their support through the coming months of grieving and finding their footing in their new lives. The rabbi said a prayer, and declared them "unmarried."

While a number of their friends and family members still did not fully understand or approve, some said that the ritual helped them to accept the new reality and to support both David and Jenna through this painful time. One of David's sisters refused to come to the ritual as she was very angry at Jenna and was attacking her repeatedly on Facebook for "cheating on her husband and then abandoning him."

David tried to deflect this hostility by making numerous posts explaining that there was no cheating, reiterating that he and Jenna were fully in agreement about their decision to divorce, and stating that they intended to remain life-long friends.

Victor and Aurora experienced a slightly different set of public relations problems. Victor says, "We both knew from the start that we should not get married, but we gave in to pressure from our families. Partly, we didn't want to get married because we were poly, and hoped to create a triad or foursome eventually. But we also knew we shouldn't get married because our relationship was too new, and we both suspected that we would not be ideal partners in the long run. Both sets of parents are immigrants from Eastern Europe and very traditional. Aurora accidentally got pregnant about one year into our dating relationship, and both sets of parents insisted that we immediately get married and move in together. We were not ready for that level of commitment, and yet we both knew we wanted children, so it seemed to make sense to go along with this program. We loved each other very much, we came from similar backgrounds, and we each felt that no one else had ever 'gotten' us the way the other did. However, even though we had some good sexual chemistry at the beginning, suddenly we were having sleepless nights with a new baby, and for me, the stresses of being the breadwinner that first year while Aurora was breastfeeding definitely took its toll on sex and romance.

"Things were just getting back to normal when we met Alia, who fell madly in love with Aurora and was also attracted to me. We went way too fast and had her move in with us within six months of meeting her, because she was in a bad housing situation and she was helping out a lot with our daughter, Fiona. It seemed practical, but was a disastrous mistake. Ironically, our parents were okay with this because 'back in the old country' all the men have 'mistresses' and the women have very low legal and financial status there, and apparently accept their husbands having a lover, so this looked fairly normal to them.

"By this time, Aurora had gone back to work part-time, but she and Alia were home together a lot while I was at work, and they really bonded and began to shut me out. Our parents absolutely refused to believe that Alia and Aurora were in a relationship. In fact, I was rapidly becoming a sidepiece in their world. The families distorted everything because they had no context for a lesbian relationship. After about a year, Alia demanded a monogamous relationship with Aurora, and was barely speaking to me. Aurora did not want to split up with me, but we both had to admit that we were no longer in love, and that the situation was untenable.

"Aurora somehow felt compelled to go along with Alia's demands, so we announced to our families that we were filing for divorce. They hit the roof, because it was fine with them to have 'my mistress' living with us, but divorce was against their beliefs and their culture, and no one else in either of our families had ever divorced. We spent years trying to explain this to our families and they were completely unable to comprehend. Aurora's parents still refuse to believe that she is in a lesbian relationship and insist that Alia is just a friend and live-in nanny. My father sat me down numerous times to ask me how on Earth I could divorce my wife when she was so compliant in allowing my 'concubine' to live with us. He just won't believe that *she* divorced *me*, it's so totally outside his life experience for a woman to divorce her husband, so I can't get through to him."

Victor has one family member who was very supportive. "One of my sisters was the only one who had a clue, because she is a nurse and has coworkers who are lesbians, so she totally gets that. But otherwise I felt very alone, very judged, and very misunderstood and ostracized by my family. And my in-laws viciously attacked me over and over again on social media, calling me an evil bastard who abandoned his wife and child, portraying Aurora as the injured party, when the reality is that Aurora divorced me to appease Alia."

Many poly people have described feeling similarly alone and isolated from family and friends, right when they need them the most. Because most people around them have never seen an open relationship before, it can be very challenging to explain these relationships even when everything is going great, and even more difficult to talk about the demise of a relationship.

George says, "At least my family responded with a mixture of confusion and relief when our triad broke up, rather than outright hostility. The whole situation was probably doomed from the start, because my partners, Gabriella and Marjorie, were both vilified by their whole families both during the relationship and afterwards.

Gabriella and I had been together for three years when we met Marjorie, and when she moved in with us, Gabriella's family showed up at our home and tried to stage an intervention. They literally thought she had lost her mind to 'let that homewrecker into your house!' Marjorie's family was irate that she was 'settling for a man who doesn't even respect you enough to leave his girlfriend and marry you.' They were convinced she must be on drugs, and her father even accused me of being a pimp! We had no idea how hard it would be to conduct a triad relationship with such intense disapproval from our families, because both my family and Gabriella's had always showered us with acceptance, love, and gifts, taking us on expensive vacations and giving us a loan to buy our house, until we got involved with Marjorie."

George's coworker Jason, an older gay man, was the only person in his life who understood what he was going through, and was very supportive. When George expressed shock and bewilderment about the family dramas, Jason gently explained, "You didn't realize that you were enjoying all that heterosexual privilege of being 'normal,' and doing the societally expected thing of settling down in a monogamous, heteronormative relationship. Your family's unconditional love and approval really props up a relationship, and when they suddenly withdraw it and ostracize you, it really puts a lot of strain on any relationship."

George acknowledges, "You're not really aware of your privilege until you lose it. It was quite humbling to see how dependent we were on the support of our families, because we are political activists who considered ourselves unconventional hipsters. Clearly we were more traditional than we thought, at least in our relationships with our families and our desire for their acceptance and approval."

Ironically, the triad's relationship ended largely because they weren't really compatible to live together. They had very different attitudes about housework, cooking, careers, and money. Marjorie was a lawyer who worked a lot of hours and made more money than George and Gabriella combined. Marjorie started to lose respect for both George and Gabriella because they barely made enough money to make their house payments, and their car got repossessed when they bounced a check for the payment. Marjorie's criticisms made George realize that he had allowed Gabriella's bad habits around money to push them to the brink of bankruptcy. Trying to talk about these financial issues highlighted glaring communication problems between George and Gabriella. And they were both unhappy with Marjorie because she didn't cook or do housework. She wanted to order takeout every night and hired a cleaner to take care of the chores.

Despite their differences, the three separated amicably, and were able to remain friends. Gabriella says, "Because all three families were attacking us, we clung together through the breakup and presented a united front. The reality was that we did really love each other. We had just asked Marjorie to move in when we were all in the pink glow of NRE, and it wasn't anyone's fault that we didn't live happily ever together." Marjorie had a lot of savings, so she helped them all financially during the transition. This allowed George to keep the house and pay back his parents for the down payment, and he found a roommate to help pay the mortgage. Marjorie bought a condo and invited Gabriella to temporarily move in with her while she got on her feet financially. They developed a closer friendship without what Marjorie called "the distraction and background noise" of trying to make the triad work. They confided to each other that they both wanted to continue some kind of romantic and sexual relationship with George, but Gabriella said, "I just don't want to live with *any* partner right now!" George was pleasantly surprised that both women eventually resumed what he described as a "dating" relationship with him, each of them seeing him about once a week for sex and companionship. He says, "And now our families are even more confused by the new arrangement! You should have seen the look on my mother's face when I told her that I have relationships with both Gabriella and Marjorie again. I thought her head was going to explode! And now our families disapprove even *more*, but we no longer care what they think."

Being in an open relationship is likely to provoke some disapproval by others. Since many people around you will not understand or accept your poly relationships while they are thriving, they are likely to have even more judgments about a relationship's demise. Some poly people minimize this by keeping their relationships private, so there is less conflict with friends, family members, coworkers, and neighbors over this issue.

However, this can be a two-edged sword. On the one hand, if you have kept your poly lifestyle secret from everyone else in your life, they can't criticize or ridicule you when your relationship ends. On the other hand, if they never even knew about that relationship, you will not have the option of asking them to be there for you during a breakup.

Margo says, "Miller and I presented ourselves to the world as a monogamous, heterosexual, married couple, mainly because Miller's long-time girlfriend, Hannah, was a minister and she felt she might lose her job if the truth came out. We also felt our kids were too young to understand and it was easy to be discreet. He could go on dates after the kids went to sleep at 8 PM.

"However, eventually Hannah's husband insisted that they go back to monogamy, and she had to split up with Miller. They were both devastated, but because no one else knew about the relationship, they had no one to turn to for support except me. I was practically becoming their therapist, fielding daily calls from Hannah crying on the phone for hours, and spending my evenings taking care of Miller because he was so sad and angry about the breakup."

CHAPTER FIFTEEN:

Is There a Better Way?

Does a Poly Breakup Really Need to Be So Horrible?

Many people have asked, "Isn't there a better way to end a poly relationship without such pain and acrimony?" The short and grossly oversimplified answer is "sometimes." As in monogamous relationships that come to an end, there are all kinds of people and situations that lead to the demise of poly relationships.

There are some factors that may significantly reduce the suffering. The key to a civilized breakup is that both parties have demonstrated reasonable levels of honesty and kindness throughout the relationship, and have behaved pretty well during the breakup. Another important variable is whether both people made efforts to solve the problems in the relationship before making the decision to end it altogether. Probably even more central to a low-drama and less painful breakup is that both people are able to see that there are specific areas of incompatibility that have caused a lot of conflict in the relationship. It's also much easier if both people have gotten past the honeymoon period, and are able to realistically see each other and the relationship. If one person is still in the grips of NRE, and believes this partner is the perfect love of their life, they are going to fight like hell against any move to end the romance.

Dissolving a love relationship should not automatically be viewed as a failure. Many couples have reported that being in a polyamorous relationship gave them insight into their problems and helped them transition into happier and healthier relationships. Many poly people believe that ending some relationships is actually healthy. Drew explains, "Some poly relationships *should* end. That's one of the great things about open relationships. You can get involved with people who are really great people and have fantastic love affairs with them. But they don't have to be totally compatible with you, because you aren't expecting them to meet all your needs, and you aren't marrying them, so it's not such a tragedy if you end up breaking up because those conflicts and incompatibilities eventually become too much. It's never going to be painless losing someone you love, but if you know from the start that you are not destined to become life partners, you can have a great relationship and not feel suicidal when it's over."

Jane says, "No matter how painful the breakup is, if you're poly, you are not as dependent on that one person for all the love in your life, so you may be able to more graciously let go of them as a lover. You have a better chance of keeping them as a friend, since you probably have another partner to provide love, affection, sex, and the other things you no longer have with them, and you are not feeling as hurt and resentful over that."

Merry says, "People are always talking about 'protecting' their relationships, but that just means they are trying to control things because they are afraid of personal growth and taking risks. Risking losing the relationship is a *good* thing—it means you are alive and your relationship is growing. Holding onto a relationship that is painful and no longer working is not really protecting anyone."

Dr. Elisabeth Sheff's Theory of Polyaffectivity

Research published by Dr. Elisabeth Sheff in 2016 indicates that polyamorous relationships may be more resilient than monogamous relationships, because they allow more options for sustaining an enduring connection and ongoing friendship even if the sex and romance is no longer part of that relationship. In her article, "Not Necessarily Broken: Redefining Success When Polyamorous Relationships End," she writes, "My data indicates that poly relationships may not last in the traditional sense of permanently retaining the same form. Instead, some poly relationships appear to last more durably than many monogamous relationships because they can flex to meet different needs over time in a way that monogamous relationships—with their abundant norms and requirements of sexual fidelity—find more challenging. While the familiar and well-explored structure monogamy provides can foster a comforting predictability, it can also constrain the meanings available to people who engage in monogamous relationships ... The scarcity of these role models frees people in polyamorous relationships to create new meanings and innovate alternative roles that better suit their unique lives. A polyamorous identity framework provides the flexible and abundant relationship choices that a conventional monogamous identity, with its firmly defined roles and well-explored models, cannot."

While sex and romance have been seen as the defining characteristics of both monogamous and polyamorous relationships, Dr. Sheff describes "a quieter version of poly identity, polyaffectivity," which she defines as "intimacy among non-sexual participants linked by poly relationships, which is more durable and flexible—able to supersede, coexist with, and outlast sexual interaction." She says, "Relationships that have such a multitude of options for interaction and define emotional intimacy as more significant than sexual intimacy provide poly people with a wide selection of possible outcomes." This outlook allows relationships to shift from lovers to friends without anyone being at fault, and relieves the pressure on couples to stay together in exactly the same way at all costs.

"Once it becomes clear that the relationship no longer meets participants' needs or works for people who have grown apart, accepting the change and shifting to accommodate new realities can contribute to more graceful endings and transitions. When people are able to amicably end one phase of their relationship, it increases the changes they will be able to make the transition to a new phase characterized by continued connection, communication, and cooperation," Dr. Sheff states. While that's all very brilliant, if it sounds like a lot of academic mumbo jumbo to you, here is a simpler explanation from one of the participants in her study: "Don't drag it out until the bitter end, disemboweling each other along the way. Split up while you can still be friends, before anybody does something they will regret later.

Dr. Sheff reminds us that our longer life spans have made lifelong monogamy with one mate unrealistic for many, because living until 85 or 90 creates a lot more time to for us to change and grow apart. A hundred years ago, when a lot of people dropped dead by age 40, it was a lot more plausible for couples to stay together "until death do us part." For at least the past 50 years, serial monogamy has largely replaced "actual" monogamy, since very few people actually marry as virgins and remain sexually exclusive with one person for their entire lives.

Dr. Sheff says, "As a social pattern, serial monogamy inevitably creates some families with multiple parents related to children through various legal, biological, and emotional connections. Parents who used to be romantic partners often end up trying to figure out how to create a workable co-parental relationship when they were unable to create or sustain a spousal relationship. For the many people in this situation, remaining on positive terms with a former partner/current co-parent makes the transition less painful for children and more cooperative for adults."

Her study reveals many examples of poly marriages and long-term love relationships that at some point evolved into platonic friendships that have endured the test of time. These transitions often allow poly families to continue raising children together, often under the same roof, without the usual joint child custody and financial consequences of separation or divorce.

In my private practice, I work primarily with LGBT clients. LGBT/queer relationships have always demonstrated more flexibility than heterosexual ones in providing models for romantic partners to transition to platonic friends and family members. This is seen by most LGBT folks as a better option than losing the relationship completely when the sex and romance ends. Any gay man "of a certain age" can share true tales of heroic ex-lovers who spent years taking care of former partners who were ill and disabled with HIV/AIDS, in many cases providing housing and financial support.

Gary and his partner, Marvin, didn't hesitate to take Marvin's former partner, Matt, and his husband, George, into their home when Matt was diagnosed with AIDS-related lymphoma and George quit his job to take care of him round the clock. Gary and Marvin both worked full-time and paid all the bills, and each took shifts taking care of Matt so George could get some rest. When Matt passed away, they invited George to continue living with them as a roommate, as they had become family to each other. Gary jokingly calls them "three dysfunctional old queens in a non-sexual triad" because many of their poly friends assumed they were in a triad together. They socialized together, had all their meals together, and even went on vacations together. Whenever they met new people who were confused by their relationship, Gary would explain, "Marvin is my husband and George is my husband's ex-husband's husband and widow."

Many other gay men can recount times when they took in ex-partners who were down on their luck, out of work, or recovering from drug or alcohol addiction. James describes driving with his husband, Brendan, to corner his ex-lover, Karl, in the back room of a gay leather bar where he was snorting speed. James and Brendan forcibly wrestled him into the car and drove him to a drug rehab center. James and Brendan paid for a month-long stay, and then had Karl move into their apartment for six months to prevent him from moving back in with his abusive boyfriend (who happened to be a speed dealer), and to help him get back on his feet.

Tony Bravo writes a column for the *San Francisco Chronicle* every Sunday that is focused on fashion, cultural trends, and relationships. One of his columns in August of

2016 was called "When In Need, I Have An Ex For That!" which was about all of his ex-boyfriends, and how lucky he is to have been able to remain good friends with them. He says not only is it great to have such a wonderful circle of friends who know him very well, but many of his exes have come through for him in times of crisis. For instance, when he has a medical problem, Tony calls an ex-partner who is a doctor to get medical advice. On another occasion, he ran into some legal problems and called an ex who is an attorney. When his best gal pal had her heart set on buying a new dress that had sold out, he called his fashion designer ex-boyfriend, who was able to find one more of the dress for her. He wrote in the column that whenever he needs help for almost any problem, "I have an ex for that!" His advice on staying friends after the breakup is, "If you want better ex-boyfriend prospects, start by picking better boyfriend prospects." He adds, "A relationship doesn't have to be till death do us part to be successful. A relationship can be a success if you take something from it. The best thing I've taken from it is the men themselves."

And many lesbians have at least one, sometimes two or three, ex-partners who remain lifelong friends and family members, often spending holidays together, becoming godmothers to each other's children, and helping each other provide care for aging parents or ill spouses. Older LGBT people came of age during an era when most queer people were shunned and rejected by their biological families, so ex-spouses often became their "real" family members, and part of a tight-knit community.

Younger LGBT people are much more likely to be accepted by and welcomed to participate in their biological families, so many do not feel as strong a need to keep former partners in their support network. But many younger LGBT people, both monogamous and poly, have continued the tradition of transitioning from lovers to close friends.

Tanya says, "I knew Megan and I could not continue as lovers, but I knew she was part of my tribe, and that I would always want her in my life. We each fell in love with new women within a year after our separation. Having new partners helped us stay friends without making the mistake of trying to get back together, which we had already tried twice before! Luckily, she and her new girlfriend live a few miles from us, and she still has the dog we raised together as a puppy. So I always use the excuse that I need to go over to see the dog, and that way I still see Megan several times a week while I am ostensibly coming over to visit the dog. My wife and I take care of the dog when they go on vacation, and they watch our house and water the garden when we go away. We sometimes spend holidays together since our families live far away, and in a weird way, the four of us really are a family."

When Isa's wife, Eileen, became disabled with multiple sclerosis, their two kids were six and 10 years old. Eileen's ex-wife, Geri, had already been "Aunt Geri" to the kids all their lives. She says, "Suddenly I was promoted to being an additional parent, since Eileen could no longer drive, cook, or keep up with the kids and their many activities." Isa repeatedly checked in with Geri, asking her "Are you sure you want this responsibility? Are you sure you have time for all this?" Geri says, "It never crossed my mind to say no! Eileen and her family had been like a surrogate family to me, and I was in the delivery room when those kids were born. I was single for 10 years after we split up, and I would have been so lonely and isolated without them in my life. They always tell everyone how I'm such a saint to take care of their kids, but the truth is that my relationship with the kids and with Eileen and Isa has absolutely enriched my life. And I always knew that if I had been the one with an illness, they would have been there for me."

Eve Rickert and Franklin Veaux, authors of *More Than Two,* are also strong proponents of building enough flexibility into poly relationships to allow them to change and grow as needed. They say, "Since people change all the time, we can debate whether it even makes sense to make lifelong commitments, at least the way society encourages us to. We're taught that marriage should mean our relationship never changes, rather than meaning we can be family for life but the shape the family takes can change." They suggest that couples stop and re-evaluate their relationships every couple of years, and "think of this as renewing the relationship." That evaluation may mean considering changes, including changing the form of the relationship from lovers to something else. "It's not the shape of the relationship that's important; it's whether it meets your needs," they say. And, sometimes a relationship is not healthy anymore: "Good relationships promote the long-term happiness and well-being of the people involved; when that no longer becomes possible, and there's no clear path to making it possible, then it might be time for the relationship to end." Rickert and Veaux acknowledge that many of these transitions involve pain and grieving, because you are experiencing the loss of romantic love and the dreams and hopes you shared for that relationship.

Rickert and Veaux add another reason to keep a friendship with your ex-partners, or at least an amicable acquaintanceship. The poly community in any given city or geographical area is usually a pretty small place, so it is very likely that you and your former lover will be running into each other at poly events, support groups, and parties for many years to come. If you burn your bridges with an ex-partner, this is likely to lead to many very awkward and uncomfortable social situations where you have to share space with them. And many people start to avoid any poly-related event or group because they *might* run into their ex, so they become more isolated and are cut off from needed sources of support.

Rickert and Veaux add an additional word of caution, "In the era of social media, it's incredibly tempting to seek validation online. We recommend keeping your breakups off social media, even if your partner doesn't follow this advice. Taking a breakup onto the world stage, especially when you are dealing with the 'anger' part of grief, has a way of backfiring. Remember, the poly community is small, and the people you force to witness your breakups will probably be your pool of potential partners later."

If you post something online at a moment of sadness, rage, or paranoia, large numbers of people are likely to see it immediately. You are likely to end up feeling embarrassed about it later, and even then, it is pretty hard to erase anything completely once it is anywhere on the internet. I have seen many clients going through bruising breakups and posting all kinds of extreme accusations and tirades.

Coraline says, "I was acting out of a desire to hurt my ex-husband as much as he hurt me. When you are in that state of feeling victimized, you think, I have to post something to tell everyone what an evil bastard he is and all the rotten things he did to me! A few days later, remorse and regret set in, and I was horrified by my own behavior. I had to do a lot of damage control to try to clean up the mess. Instead of hurting him, I came off as this psycho hose beast, and everyone was emailing John saying things like, 'Now I understand why you are divorcing her.' So while I was hoping to generate sympathy and show how awful and wrong he was, it totally backfired on me and made me look like a complete idiot."

One way of easing this process is to consider a period of no-contact with your ex until you both can get through the process of grieving the loss of the romantic relationship. That reduces the likelihood of either of you saying (or posting) anything that will cause irreparable damage, and that you will almost certainly regret. And it is likely to make it easier to build a long-term friendship once the anger and sadness have subsided.

Dawn Davidson is a life coach, polyamory educator, and author of the book *KISSable Agreements*. On her website, loveoutsidethebox.com, she provides a very useful article called "Is It Over?" to help people decide whether it is time to end a relationship. She quotes Richard Bach's description of his very loving and amicable divorce, and his lifelong friendship with his former wife. He believes he and his wife were, "…led to find each other, led through the years we lived together, and led to part. When a marriage comes to an end, we're free to call it a failure. We're also free to call it a graduation."

Rashi and George were a heterosexual couple going through a divorce. When they read Bach's quote, each had very different reactions. Rashi said, "Well, that gives me hope! It's really encouraging to know that some couples can become friends after splitting up, and can see their divorce as a natural evolution to some other kind of relationship." George responded bitterly, "What kind of drugs is that guy on? How can he possibly be calling something as ugly and painful as a divorce a 'graduation?'" Clearly, it is quite difficult for most people to look at a divorce or separation through such a positive and philosophical lens until they have gone through the grieving process and reached some amount of acceptance of the new reality. The majority of romantic relationships, both monogamous and polyamorous, end with some suffering and sadness, but with a lot of effort and the passage of time, some people have found ways to make the process less painful.

Some Positive Examples of "Graceful Distancing"

One peculiarly poly method of breaking up is the slow, gradual drifting apart and disappearing from each other's lives, or of shifting from romantic partners to platonic friends. During the late 1960s through the 1980s, there were several polyamorous communal families in San Francisco that were called Kerista communes. The Keristans practiced polyfidelity, a form of heterosexual group marriage. They called a gradual transition from lovers to friends "graceful distancing," meaning spending less and less time together and being less sexual and affectionate until a couple are no longer lovers, and then can either decide to be friends or just stop seeing each other altogether. Because it is not abrupt and dramatic, it gives both people time to naturally start spending more time with other lovers or friends, gradually rebuilding their support system, and adding more affection and sex with other people so they do not experience a scarcity of love and attention.

In a monogamous relationship, this method is usually intolerably painful, as each partner is acutely aware of the lack of companionship, emotional intimacy, and sex. In a poly relationship, each person is free to pursue new partners or spend more time with other existing partners to ease the transition. Monogamous people do not have this option, so they usually find it very lonely and heartbreaking to slowly lose their beloved. Even for poly people, this only works if both people feel highly motivated to cooperate with the incremental plan. Some people find this torturous, and would rather just break up immediately and get it over with.

Sometimes, both people in the couple can see that they are incompatible and can both find more appropriate partners. For instance, Lelieni and Garth were both bisexual, and through opening up their marriage and having other lovers, they discovered that they were each more oriented towards same-sex relationships than they had previously believed. However, they really loved each other as companions and enjoyed owning a home together. Garth's lover, Alfredo, lived a few blocks away, so Garth started spending a lot of time at Alfredo's place. Leilieni's partner, Krisha, moved in with her full-time. Leilieni and Garth split up as a romantic couple but continued living together. All four of them were much happier once Lelieni and Garth acknowledged that their relationship as lovers was transitioning to a friendship. Garth says, "It seemed to evolve organically. Polyamory allowed each relationship to become what it actually should be. Before that we were trying to force each of our relationships into a box where they just didn't fit. We had thought we were primary partners and that the outside lovers were secondary, The truth of the matter was that we were destined to be best friends and family to each other, and those so-called outside lovers were in fact our life partners."

Sharon and Bruce are a heterosexual married couple, who both became seriously involved with outside partners. They loved living together and their house was a social gathering place "for all of our misfit geek and Goth friends" for parties, movie nights, and gaming. Bruce says, "One day we looked up and realized that we were no longer romantic partners. We loved each other just as much as ever and were extremely close, but our bond had become platonic, and luckily we both were able to admit that. From the start of our relationship, we were very affectionate and had good sex, but the real bond between us was the emotional closeness and intellectual rapport. We decided to stay married because it helps our tax situation, and I can get health benefits through her job. We have continued to live together part-time but we each spend more nights than not with the other partners, and the shift has been relatively painless. It really helps that all our friends have supported both of us through this, and have not seen this as a 'tragic end' to a marriage. They can see that we are happy, and ironically, to them it looks like nothing has changed, since we still live together and spend a lot of time together and are still constantly hosting parties together at the house."

Jane and her husband, Rodrigo, had a different experience, but a similarly painless transition. "We slowly became more distant as lovers because our life paths and goals had diverged," Jane says. "You want to be able to grow, and you want your partner to be allowed that same evolution. But when you give each other that freedom, there's no guarantee that you will stay on the same path. And really, what's the alternative? Trying to force yourself and your spouse to stay the same forever? I'm not the same person I was 25 years ago, when we first met. We were both 22, going to school, and working as bartenders till 3 AM. I followed my dreams to become a working artist and political activist, and Rodrigo's been on a much different path, founding a successful tech company. His priorities are making money and having a house and kids, and I admire and respect him, but that is definitely not for me.

"We're both a lot happier now that we have divorced, and found partners who are right for us. If we had not opened up our marriage and started outside relationships, we would probably still be fighting a losing battle, each trying to guilt-trip the other person to do what *we* want, instead of what is right for them. And we'd both be absolutely miserable."

Mina and Marco are a married couple who experienced some tensions in their relationship, primarily because both of their families disapproved of their relationship. When Mina called her family in Sri Lanka and told them she and Marco had gotten engaged, the entire family freaked out.

Her father cried, "I can't believe you're marrying a Mexican!" even though he knew that Marco was Puerto Rican-American and his family had lived in New York City for over a century. And when Marco called his family in New York to announce that he was marrying Mina, his mother shrieked, "He's marrying some Hindu girl from India," although she had been told repeatedly that Mina was Muslim and from Sri Lanka. Mina's father even enlisted one of her brothers to fly from Sri Lanka to San Diego to try to prevent their wedding, and to try to get Mina to "come back home." Mina's grandfather scolded her mother, "I *told* you not to let her go to medical school in America! Look what happened!"

With all this going on, they chose not to tell their families that they had a polyamorous relationship. Mina and Marco had a mutual boyfriend who spent every weekend with them. Bruno is a chef at an upscale restaurant, and also Puerto Rican-American. Marco jokes that if only their families were not homophobic, they would consider them a perfect match, and that his mother would probably say, "At least he's Catholic!" Marco and Bruno have a very strong romantic and emotional connection, partly growing out of their similar working-class upbringing in what Bruno called, "families that could be completely dysfunctional in both English and Spanish."

While Mina shared a sexual and romantic relationship with Bruno, she felt shut out of the men's intense friendship, saying, "I'm so jealous of your bro-mance!" Bruno gradually realized that he was more gay than bisexual and that he was "emotionally monogamous." He enjoyed having casual male sex partners, but could not really sustain the relationship with Mina. Mina and Bruno gradually transitioned to a more platonic relationship by spending less and less time together, as Bruno became romantically exclusive with Marco. The breakup was pretty painless, but Mina disliked being excluded every weekend, when Bruno and Marco seemed focused only on each other. She asked Marco to spend one weekend a month alone with her, and spend one weekend night with her on the other weekends. They were able to negotiate a compromise: Bruno was able to change his schedule at the restaurant to have Sundays and Mondays off from work to spend with Marco, who is self-employed and could arrange his own work schedule. As a result, Mina could have every Friday night and all day Saturdays with Marco. She was able to navigate the breakup with Bruno, and accept his continued relationship with Marco, because her needs for time, love, and for feeling included were being met.

Being able to treat each other well and having mutual respect is a key factor in amicable poly breakups. Akiko and Mollie separated after living together for five years, and Akiko expressed surprise and relief that they were able to transition to a platonic friendship "without hating each other." She had previously survived a brutal heterosexual divorce. Her husband lied about an affair with another woman, which only came out after he had given Akiko herpes. The deception and betrayal had caused her suicidal anguish and homicidal rage, causing her to check herself into a psychiatric hospital "to prevent me from killing myself or killing him." The contrast in this separation was striking. Akiko says, "Because Mollie had always treated me like a queen and been honest and communicative about everything, we were able to end our relationship with dignity and without attacking each other. It was sad to give up on my dream of growing old with her, but I had to admit that she was right. We had tried everything and we weren't really happy together. I feel certain that we will be lifelong friends, so in some sense we will grow old together, just not as lovers. And because she didn't leave me *for* someone else, but because we really couldn't work things out ourselves, I did not feel rejected and abandoned.

"We had been polyamorous the whole time we lived together, and ironically, that had nothing to do with our breakup. That part of our relationship was going great! In fact, it helped a lot that I had recently started a new love affair, which I knew would not be long-term, but some hot sex and romance really distracted me from the feelings of sadness and loss about Mollie splitting up with me."

Martin and Kiara had lived together for four years in the south side of Chicago, in the neighborhood where they had both grown up. They lived just a few blocks from both sets of parents, and because Kiara's father was a Baptist minister, they were under intense pressure to get married. Their families did not know that they had an open relationship, which included Martin having a girlfriend, Lila, and Kiara also having a girlfriend, Cecilia. They took great pains to be discreet about these outside relationships because their parents lived nearby, and because Kiara did not want to cause her father any problems with his church.

When Lila unexpectedly became pregnant, Martin and Kiara asked her to move in with them so they could raise the baby together. They moved to a larger apartment in the same building, so they could have two bedrooms, one for Kiara and one for Lila. Martin spent alternate nights with each partner. This "forced us out of the closet," Martin explains, and required weathering some family drama. Martin's parents were community organizers who had named him after Dr. Martin Luther King, Jr., and his father had several "man-to-man talks" with him about how he was embarrassing his family by "acting so ghetto," and "shacking up with two women and having babies without getting married." Kiara's parents went ballistic, trying to force her to "leave that no-good cheater" and move back home with them. Before the baby was even born, Lila's mother threatened to go to court to get custody, "Because ALL FOUR of you kids are crazy!" Kiara's lover, Cecilia, knew a gay, male therapist with expertise in open relationships, and he provided couples' counseling and family therapy to help all four of them through this crisis.

All of them loved their families very much, and felt a lot of guilt about disappointing them. But they were determined to be good parents and good partners. Cecilia also connected them with a family law attorney who drew up some legal documents to provide clarity about who had what legal rights related to custody of the baby.

They stood their ground, and when their beautiful baby girl was born, she stole everyone's hearts, and all the parents and grandparents managed to reconcile. Lila's mother remarked, "This girl is going to be the most spoiled child on the planet—she has three moms, a father, and two sets of grandparents all doting on her!"

Despite the seeming harmony, over the next year Martin and Kiara's relationship started to unravel. He was sleeping in Lila's room nearly every night in order to help with the frequent feeding and diaper changes. Kiara felt that Lila and Martin "behaved like a married couple," and because of the baby, they got all the recognition as a couple from all the families. When the baby was about three months old, Cecilia's mother suddenly needed surgery, and Cecilia stayed at her mother's house on the other side of Chicago for a few months to take care of her. Kiara felt abandoned by both Martin and Cecilia. She felt completely displaced as Martin's partner, even though he reassured her that once the baby started sleeping through the night, things would be back to normal.

However, when Martin tried to start sleeping in Kiara's room again, Lila was distraught and accused him of "abandoning his child," and leaving her with all the work of taking care of the baby. Frequent arguments ensued between Martin and both Kiara and Lila, and the two women started having disputes about everything from dirty dishes to who was paying more bills. Try as he might, Martin could not make either partner happy. Kiara's mother could see how unhappy she was and started pressuring her to leave Martin, quoting Bible verses about adultery, and shaming her for "putting up with a man who has a baby with another woman."

After the baby's first birthday, Kiara decided to temporarily move in with Cecilia to think things over. After a few months, they decided to become a primary couple. Ironically, Kiara's parents became even more distraught, as they had convinced themselves that Cecilia was "just a friend." Kiara had come out to her parents about her bisexuality at least a few times, and had introduced Cecelia to them as her lover, but, "As long as I was living with Martin, they didn't believe me." At first Martin tried to win Kiara back, promising to be more attentive to her needs. However, he quickly realized that life was much less stressful without the constant conflicts between the three of them, and he reluctantly accepted her decision to end the relationship.

Kiara and Martin still loved and cared for each other, and were very motivated to continue with a platonic friendship. Because they each had another primary partner, the transition from lovers to friends went relatively smoothly. And since Kiara and Cecilia had both established a strong relationship with the baby, they continued to be what Lila called "the fairy godmothers," frequently babysitting to give the parents a much-needed break. Lila and Kiara became friends again once the romantic rivalry was resolved, with Lila joking, "Martin was the problem child, not Kiara." Five years later, Cecilia and Kiara had a baby, and Lila and Martin became the godparents. The various sets of grandparents are all still shaking their heads in confusion and disapproval, but have grudgingly accepted that this unconventional blended family is here to stay.

Jerome and Peggy divorced after 15 years of marriage and a 10-year struggle with infertility. They both finally accepted that they could not conceive a child together, but the disappointment, exhaustion, and tensions caused by the costs of infertility treatments finally destroyed their relationship. They each had another partner who had supported them through the long grieving process of not having a baby, and those partners now helped them through their divorce.

Jerome says, "I think Peggy and I both behaved honestly and honorably through it all. We had developed good communication skills and relationship skills from poly books and workshops, which served us well in trying to work through the struggle with infertility. Ironically, by the time we split up, we were pretty good at working together on problems." Peggy says, "We couldn't stand living together any more, as our home had become this place where we were miserable together. We had stopped having sex at least a year before we separated, because sex had become so fraught with anxiety about trying to get pregnant. It was his idea to divorce, but it really was the only option. Because we had both treated each other with kindness and respect throughout the marriage, we were able to continue that way through the divorce. I don't know what kind of friendship we will be able to have from here, but we do love each other and want to have some connection.

"Thank goodness we each have another partner to help us. I was literally suicidal when I finally had to admit I would never be able to have a child, and our partners have been so compassionate and supportive."

Jerome adds, "It's actually humorous because I was the one who was initially reluctant to have an open marriage and Peggy was really pushing it. Now I have become such an advocate, and I call myself a 'poly cheerleader' because being poly has totally come through for me at the very worst time of my life."

These are some of the possibilities for polyamorous relationships to end with less pain. The odds of a "successful" breakup are much higher if both people are happily engaged in other healthy relationships, as this is likely to ease the fear of scarcity and of being alone. And many people report that being able to hold onto a friendship with their partner made it much easier to let go of the romantic relationship without rancor. Several also pointed to the importance of having poly-friendly mutual friends, who were able to give both people support and assure them they would still be there despite the separation.

A graceful parting is much more possible for couples where both parties are past the intensity of the honeymoon stage of the relationship, as they are able to see the relationship and their incompatibility more clearly. Couples who have behaved lovingly, and been caring and competent partners throughout the relationship are more likely to be able to preserve that positive regard for each other and treat each other well during the breakup, significantly reducing the pain.

CHAPTER SIXTEEN:

Going Forward

Most polyamorous people who have created successful and healthy relationships will humbly acknowledge that they have had a few disastrous and painful breakups along the way. Luckily, many have learned from their mistakes and developed a skill set that has helped them select appropriate partners, and to be good partners themselves. This steep learning curve has helped them figure out what model of open relationships they want, improved their communication with partners, and given them enough practice to develop the strong interpersonal skills required for sustaining poly relationships.

This is especially true for older people who pioneered open relationships during an era when few resources existed. Buddy says, "My wife, Estelle, and I were stumbling in the dark trying to have what we called an open marriage in the 1980s and 90s, before the internet existed and there were literally no books about it, and the word "polyamory" had not been invented yet. Even though we lived in New York City, we could not find any therapist who knew anything, and, in fact, they were all very hostile to anything outside of traditional monogamy and said we must be sex addicts or mentally ill to even be trying this."

Estelle says, "I have a lot of regrets because I fell in love with a married man, and his wife eventually divorced him because she decided she wanted monogamy. I have apologized to her for the pain this caused her, and tried to make amends, but the reality is that we had no idea what we were doing, and no one to give us any guidance. My lover is still with me, and he is living with us now. Of course he was devastated when his wife left him, but he says he knows now that they could never be happy together because he is polyamorous by nature.

"My husband also has a really wonderful 20-year relationship with his other partner, and our marriage continues to be strong."

Buddy says, "It's amazing to me that now there are poly Meetup groups, therapists, websites, blogs, and potlucks. So poly people now have some help to avoid a lot of the mistakes we made. I had a girlfriend for several years during the 1990s, and one day she suddenly got this look of horror on her face and said, 'You and Estelle are just making this up as you go along, aren't you?' It had apparently just dawned on her that we had no road map, and were doing the best we could to make this work."

Estelle adds, "Everyone in our large poly community here in New York seems to see us as role models since we have a successful long-term marriage and happy concurrent relationships. We try to remind them that we inadvertently hurt some people along the way, because of our lack of skills and knowledge about ourselves and polyamory. We really encourage people to take the poly workshops and classes, read the books, get therapy, to utilize all the poly resources out there, so they *won't* hurt other people by being incompetent like we were."

Shane says, "I grew up in Wyoming on a cattle ranch in the early 1960's, in a very traditional rural community. Even during high school, I knew that regardless of which girl I was dating, I constantly wanted the other girls, too! I felt very guilty, and thought there must be something wrong with me, because I could never be totally satisfied with one woman.

"I moved to Chicago to go to college, and got involved in the kink/leather scene there. I met a few gay men who had multiple partners in a BDSM context of having a boyfriend, as well as having another man who was a submissive. These guys had it totally together, living in BDSM families as triads and quads, and I was so impressed with them. This made me realize I was not the only guy in the world who wanted more than one partner, and maybe I wasn't such a total freak to need that. I fell in love with two fantastic women. One was a switch, and the other was submissive, and I tried having a relationship with both of them. I royally screwed up both relationships because I didn't know how to talk about my needs and desires, or how to be completely honest and transparent about everything. I lost both of them, since I had no idea how to manage the needs and demands of two relationships, and I was constantly letting them down."

After a period of despair and introspection, Shane realized he needed help. "I couldn't find a therapist with any knowledge or expertise in open relationships, and the few therapists I talked to thought I was a drooling psychopath for being into BDSM," he says. "I started having sessions with a professional dominatrix to learn from her, and she agreed to take me on as a student and to mentor me. She taught me the skills to being a good dominant, and how to take care of a submissive, as well as how to meet the emotional needs of more than one woman. She jokingly called what she was teaching 'Kindergarten women skills for clueless straight guys.'

"As a result, I have been able to have the successful poly life I previously only dreamed of, with two committed primary relationships with two wonderful women. Each partner also has other partners, we have great communication, and everyone is pretty happy. I wish I had had some way of learning those skills before, because it would have saved me, and my previous partners, a lot of pain. But at that time, it was almost impossible to find information or tools for having open relationships."

Lise says, "It's hard to admit that you've made a mess of your relationships, but it's the first step to learning how to do it better the next time. How could any of us possibly know how to 'do' successful poly relationships? Even though I went to high school during the 1980s, it's not like they taught us *any* relationship skills in our Health or Sex Ed classes. And when I was in college you certainly didn't see a class about open relationships, or even about monogamous relationships.

"And yeah, the monogamous people mess up relationships, too, nobody gives them a clue either on how to be a good partner or how to pick the right partners. My mother sat me down around age 13 and told me to use birth control if I have sex, and told me that condoms would protect me from getting AIDS, and that was about it for any training on sex and relationships. And, being a lesbian, the advice about birth control and condoms was not very useful to me. Love relationships are very complex, and it takes years to build a poly skill set. Unfortunately we had to do it through trial and error."

Lise expresses regrets about "dragging my girlfriend through years of confusion and aggravation, because I would try so hard to be monogamous because I thought that was the only option. Then of course I would meet another irresistible woman and I would cheat, and feel guilty, and promise never to do it again." Her partner, Carinne, says, "I wish someone had sat Lise down and just told her, 'hey, it's fine to want more than one partner, it's okay, just figure out how to do it in a mature, responsible way, without driving everyone bonkers.' She went to therapists who told her she had a love addiction and needed a 12-step recovery program, but she really just needed to wake up and realize she was just *not* a monogamous chick! Duh!! She gradually learned how to be in a relationship with me, living with me and keeping her commitments to me, and also manage her time and energy well enough to have another girlfriend and keep her happy, too."

Lise adds, "If we decide to have kids, we will definitely explain to them that being monogamous or being poly are equally valid lifestyles. Nowadays, more and more parents are telling their children that being gay or straight are both okay as a sexual orientation, but I wish they would also present non-monogamy as being just as acceptable as monogamy. That could save the next generation of poly people a lot of angst."

Ray lives in a small town in the UK, about two hours from London, and he says, "I made a bloody mess of my first poly relationship because we were trying to magically create something out of whole cloth, something we had never seen and had no idea how to do." He and his partner, Chelsea, are both bisexual and they thought it would be great for two bisexual couples to live together, and create a family together. This was the early 1990s, and they didn't have the internet yet in the rural area where they lived, so they placed discreet personals ads in alternative newspapers and in newsletters of swingers clubs to meet other couples.

Through the ads, they met a married couple who lived in London. Leonard was bisexual but his wife, Hallie, was straight. They became friends and eventually lovers, and started traveling by train to spend weekends together. Ray noticed that Hallie always had several drinks before having sex with him, and because she seemed very lukewarm about it, Ray was ambivalent about pursuing a sexual relationship with her. Ray and Leonard tended to have a lot of sex because they were quite enthusiastic about each other. Chelsea started to feel ignored and left out. She knew Hallie was straight and that they would not be having a sexual relationship, but she had expected a friendship, and was very disappointed that Hallie stayed inebriated during their weekends together and was not much of a companion. And when Chelsea and Leonard tried to have sex, Hallie had anxiety attacks and they had to stop. It became clear pretty quickly that Leonard and Ray had a fantastic relationship, but no one else in this foursome did. They gave up trying to have a "couple-to-couple relationship," and Leonard and Ray continued to meet for sex and friendship a few times a month as their schedules allowed. Chelsea was eventually able to connect with other bisexual women through an LGBT center in London that had a monthly bi women's potluck. She fell in love with a woman she met through the group, and they developed an ongoing relationship.

Chelsea says, "Things didn't turn out the way we planned, but we had no role models so we just had to stumble around trying things that didn't work, until we found the right partners and allowed things to develop more organically." Ray adds, "We had this fantasy about meeting the perfect couple and falling in love and living happily ever after, but real life is much more complicated! I mean, what is the likelihood that all four people are going to really have chemistry, and really like each other and be compatible to live together? I'm sure some people get lucky, but most probably don't! We just had to take a step back and acknowledge that Leonard and I had fallen in love and had great chemistry as well, and now that relationship has survived for 25 years. He is still married to Hallie, and she is fine with him having a relationship with a man, but doesn't want him to have any other female partners. She is much happier not participating in anything sexual with him, as it triggers too much jealousy and insecurity for her."

Many people going through the heartbreak of a poly breakup find themselves doubting whether polyamory could ever work for them, and are fearful of trying again. However, most poly people discover that once they recover from the grief of losing a beloved, they feel more hopeful. And usually they have learned a lot from the experience and have a better skill set for making their next relationship work. It's healthy and normal to mourn the end of a precious relationship, and it can shake your confidence in yourself and in your decision to pursue a polyamory life. But don't despair! Open relationships are complex and require skill and practice, and you are much more likely to be successful the next time.

Index

self-knowledge, following breakup, 176–79
serial monogamy, 7–8, 212
sexting, 16, 96, 124
sexual behaviours, agreements about, 17–19
sexually transmitted infections (STIs), 74–75, 76
sexual problems
    BDSM-orientation and, 24–25
    being poly as solution to, 19–20, 23–25
    as cause of breakups, 16–25
    desire discrepancy, 20–23
    lack of sex, 21–22, 22–23
    long-term relationships vs. new relationships, 20–21
shaming, 8, 67, 198, 226
Sheff, Dr. Elisabeth, 7, 10, 210–12
slut-shaming, 8
social media, 217–18
spontaneity, 120–28
support
    from friends, 198–99, 201, 205, 207, 216–17, 221
    lack of, 204

T
texting, 16, 124
therapy, 23, 62, 178, 180, 69, 232, 234
    see also counseling
threesomes, 37, 42, 95
time and energy management, 115–37
trust, 9, 17, 18, 75, 96

V
Veaux, Franklin and Rickert, Eve, 198, 216–17
video sex, 96, 124
violence
    characterological, 65–69
    emotional, 65–69
    rates of intimate-partner, 64
    situational, 64–65
    see also abuse
V triads, 101, 102–3

Also from Thornapple Press

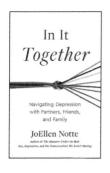

In It Together
JoEllen Notte

"JoEllen Notte takes taboo subjects,
sex and depression, and makes them
approachable for anyone ready to take
the journey. With her wit, empathy,
and knowledge, JoEllen makes it safe
to people to explore their deepest
pleasures and their biggest fears."
—Shadeen Francis, MFT

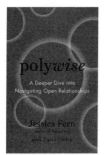

Polywise
A Deeper Dive into Navigating
Open Relationships
Jessica Fern, with David Cooley

Polywise provides both the conceptual
framework to better understand the
shift from monogamy to nonmonogamy
and the tools to navigate the next steps,
allowing you to not just survive in open
relationships, but thrive in them.

Ask Yourself:
The Consent Culture Workbook
Kitty Stryker

"When Kitty Stryker tugs on the thread of 'consent,' vast, oppressive power structures start to unravel. This workbook gets down to the fundamental principles of how humans need to treat one another. Taking its own metholology to heart, it offers no authoritative answers, just smart, emotionally astute questions that could upend how you think about the problem of other people."
—Alison Bechdel, author of *Dykes to Watch Out For* and *Fun Home*

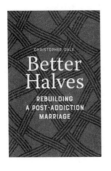

Better Halves
Christopher Dale

"A well written and prescriptive read for any person or couple navigating the trials and tribulations of addiction and recovery."
—Ryan Hampton, national addiction recovery advocate and author of *American Fix*

**Claiming the B in LGBT:
Illuminating the Bisexual Narrative**
Edited by Kate Harrad, with a
foreword by H. Sharif Williams

"With bisexuality becoming ever
more visible in mainstream culture,
this book is essential reading for bi
people and would-be allies, within
the LGBT community and beyond."
—Louise Carolin, deputy
editor, DIVA magazine

**Love's Not Color Blind:
Race and Representation
in Polyamorous and Other
Alternative Communities**
Kevin A. Patterson, with a foreword
by Ruby Bougie Johnson

"Kevin does amazing work both centering
the voices of people of color and educat-
ing white folks on privilege. His words
will positively influence polyamorous
communities for years to come."
—Rebecca Hiles, The Frisky Fairy

**Ask Me About Polyamory:
The Best of Kimchi Cuddles**
Tikva Wolf

"Kimchi Cuddles is a snapshot of our
changing culture. A warm-hearted, wise,
and brave comic: an invaluable resource
in the global polyamory movement."
—Dr. Anya, author of *Opening Love*

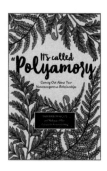

**It's Called "Polyamory":
Coming Out About Your
Nonmonogamous Relationships**
Tamara Pincus and Rebecca Hiles,
with a foreword by Kendra Holliday

"Doing poly, holding poly space
in the world, is hard work, often
thankless. Thanks to this wonderful
resource, it's now a lot easier."
—Loraine Hutchins, co-editor,
*Bi Any Other Name: Bisexual
People Speak Out*